# FINGERPRINTS
# OF
# GOD

*Fran Blackwell*

InspiringVoices®

Inspiring Voices books may be ordered through booksellers or by contacting:

Inspiring Voices
1663 Liberty Drive
Bloomington, IN 47403
www.inspiringvoices.com
1 (866) 697-5313

ISBN: 978-1-4624-1026-2 (sc)

Library of Congress Control Number: 2014913109

Printed in the United States of America.

Inspiring Voices rev. date: 08/25/2014

# Contents

# Foreword

A few years ago Fran showed me a poem she had written. We were passing by each other in a restaurant and I read it quickly on the run but knew I wanted to take time to re-read it slowly later. From a quick read I picked up a familiar style.

"This sounds like a Rumi poem," I blurted out.

"Well, he's my teacher," she said matter-of-factly, as though it were perfectly natural. I know of some people who are able to learn things such as playing a musical instrument in the dream state, by tapping into the immense inner worlds of possibility, but never had I heard of anyone being in a poetry class with Rumi, the revered 13<sup>th</sup> century Persian Sufi mystic poet. I was in awe.

Later, I thought I should have held both hands, cupped, palms up, to receive this first poem, since it was a harbinger of the many gifts her poems would bring.

Over the next year or so, the poems seemed to be literally pouring out of her. When I opened my computer in the morning, I'd find, like an overnight gift delivery, one of these spiritually astute poems in my inbox. It reminded me of a line in a poem by Tennyson: *"There she weaves by night and day, a magic web of colors gay, she has heard a whisper say....,"*

Long before I knew Fran as this poet-weaver, she was my spiritual inspiration, though I hardly knew her at the time. She is easily recognizable as one of the great Souls who emanate light, love and spiritual wisdom. I wanted to learn from her; I wanted to know what she had that made her special. When she began writing these poems, it became evident to a lot of people that these were precious messages. They let us have a glimpse into her universe, like small doors that open into a larger world. Her poems help us cross that bridge from the outer into the real worlds of truth, divine wisdom and mystery.

One morning when I was in the throes of despair over one of life's challenges, a poem was in my mailbox that addressed the very problem I was facing. It had the impact of shifting my entire outlook to a different, more positive place. This dramatic effect made me realize how deeply she was the vehicle for the wisdom of the Divine through her poetry. It showed me that her poetry is not only a literary expression of her consciousness, but a service to others who read it. The gentle words can lead to a healing place where one can be renewed and refreshed.

Like Rumi, Fran's poetry is beyond religion, culture, and time. It speaks to all who have the ears to hear and the vision to see the uncommon beauty and insight that manifests in her words. A poem like *Celebrating Your Divinity* takes an ordinary observation and gently points out the spiritual wisdom. It also bespeaks a spiritual intimacy with her Maker.

> *Canadian geese majestic riding wind currents,*
> *flap their wings and soar,*
> *Yet I beheld a moment when they decided*
> *to walk across a busy roadway,*
> *to the ire of drivers in a hurry to go*
> *no place, someplace...so the ears could*
> *only hear car horns honking,*
> *and impatience won out, and feathers flew,*
> *how sad it was, and left me to wonder why.*
> *Why were they walking across the busy roadway,*
> *When they have the gift of flight?*

*The answer came from within. Why do*
*you O Soul, walk, crawl, when you to can soar?*
*Why do you choose to turn from your radiance,*
*when you carry the light of sixteen suns?*

The poet, Archibald MacLeish said "A poem should be palpable and mute/As a globed fruit. " (*Ars Poetica*). Fran Blackwell's poetry is that strange paradox. It is at once easily accessible and yet mystically and silently profound. The joy in reading is surpassed by the joy of discovery when you recognize a gem that is especially appealing to you.

Love, Surrender and Service to all Life are the central themes in her poetry. These themes manifest stylistically from humor to ecstasy. A whimsical poem such as *The Mind is Going Down* says:

*The defeat of the mind,*
*The moment of mental waterloo*
*When it occurs with meltdown splendor,*
*Is an epic moment in the unfolding of Soul.*

*This moves Soul up on the survival scale....*
*Why is this?*
*Because,*
*A surrendered mind is a true servant...*

She turns a mystery into an insight with one carefully produced phrase.

The subject of her poetry is *Life* and each poem is like a song from the experiences of Soul. With infinite patience and acceptance, she examines the experiences of her own life and delivers the inner wisdom she gains from this examination into common language. She shares her spiritual inheritance unselfishly, honestly, joyously.

Fran Blackwell's poems will delight, surprise and give you many jewels to contemplate as they move you to a sacred space. If the sheer enormity of her poetry overwhelms, pick a line, a word, or a phrase, and focus on that. Most of all, her poetry lives up to MacLeish's famous dictum:

"For love/The leaning grasses and two lights above the sea—
A poem should not mean/But be."

Joyce G. Snyder, Author of
*The Truth About Benjamin Franklin, a novel*

## Preface

I have often wondered what it is that draws me to create poetry, and then I say, perhaps poetry creates me. Words for me have always been more that just words, they are like notes of music that create the Light and Sound of Holy Spirit, that calls to the readers' heart an awakening of their own Divinity.

The poem is the music of life and living, and as it finds expression through me, I am filled with the sacredness and gratitude that comes as a gift to my heart, for this can only happen as I listen to the voice of Spirit calling me, Soul, beyond the limitations of the mind. As this happens, words become a river of sacred blessings finding their expression in the story-telling of the divine nature in the experiences and challenges each of us as Soul goes through in life.

The words resonate within and are recognized by other Souls, and with their listening heart find strength of understanding, and an acceptance of how each experience of daily living can lead to growing, and spiritual maturity.

Words that come from an open heart, can open other hearts to the divine nature of Soul and Its purpose-- to let go of fear, to take steps on this magnificent journey of learning to love ourselves and accept the truth that *God loves Soul*. All things are possible when one finds freedom to give and receive Divine Love. It is the task of Soul to learn this truth.

And so for me, the song of poetry is not just the song of life, but the song of loving life each and every moment, with every breath, with every heartbeat, awakening in others the call of freedom and the wisdom to answer this call.

It is my hope that each poem, each word will resonate with other Souls and will help them to begin to remember the sound, light and love within themselves. Remembering this is the majesty of God's love for Soul.

When Soul discovers and learns to embrace the relationship with the Creator as a divine reality, It begins to know that it is love and love alone that clears cobwebs of illusion so the blinded eye can see and know this Presence.

Yes! See the fingerprints of God.

Fran Blackwell
April, 2014
Plantation, Florida

# Dedication

This book is lovingly dedicated to Sri Harold Klemp, my Master and Teacher and Spiritual Guide for over 40 years, and who as Z, has been my beloved companion on this Soul's journey through many lifetimes as I make my way back home to God.

Deepest gratitude and thanks to the Creator of the Sound of HU, a love song to God. Singing HU can transform your life and open your heart more fully to God's Love. HU, a single word can make a difference.

and

to Ed Blackwell, my beloved husband and renowned Jazz Drummer, who always encouraged my creativity and writing.

# Acknowledgements

Many, thanks from my heart to....

~Barbara Moss for her help, love and support.

~Edward Blackwell whose music always uplifts me, and is what I hear when I am a vehicle for the poetry.

~Rodney Jones, my friend and Brother from the ancient days, who inspires my heart to sing.

~Bob Hays, a friend of forever, whose wisdom and loving insight, causes me to take a deeper look.

~Joyce Snyder, who gives new meaning to Divine listening, and who served as a loving and skillful midwife to bring this book to life.

## The Golden Cup

Each morning I drink from the Golden Cup,
filled with the sweet nectar of consciousness,
distilled from the crucible of the Heart.
There is no longer a thirst,
for it has been quenched,
and will be quenched daily.

Beloved, I ask,
*Why do you bring me this cup*
*each morning and let me drink my fill?*

"This cup is yours, made by you,
to hold the Golden Nectar."

How did I make it I wonder...

The Beloved hears my wondering and answers:

"You forged this cup from your sweat and tears,
your truth telling,
your Divine Blessing to behold
not the things of God,
But God of ITSELF.

"But what gives this cup that you drink from
great strength and endurance,
is your capacity to love, unconditionally,
All of Life,
Just for Love,

Just because you can,
Just BE cause you know God Loves you.

Behold the Golden Cup you hold,
See the fingerprints of God.

## A Garden of Gratitude

Growing within the temple grounds of my heart,
is a garden of gratitude.
Planted with seeds of gratefulness,
tended with loving care.

Each moment, the blessings of love abound
as I remember each and every bloom blossoming
in this special garden of delight.

I am the guardian for this garden of gratitude,
making sure everything growing has been planted
with tenderness and sweetness.
For each blessing of gratitude is honored
with the deepest of prayer and understanding.

I know each seed in the passing parade of
life's moments must be caught within the heart,
open to love's song, sung in the depths of the
deepest stillness, the whirlpool where silence
speaks in quiet fulfillment of the ancient promise--
God Loves me-Soul,
and like a dandelion gone to seed,
blown out on the breath of Holy Spirit,
they fly into the wind finding fertile ground,
to nourish their sprouting into grateful moments,
taking root in my Garden of Gratitude.

Blessings of light and sound; forever on holy ground,
for when I pray, I am listening to God.

All the blessings, for which I am grateful,
is God showing me how deeply He listens?
The wavelength of communication
is the language of Gratitude,
spoken on wings of love, holy listening,
softness falls into open hearts,
open arms, love's embrace, opened eyes, softened by tears,
open-minded in agreement to serve Soul.

Beautiful, glorious Soul, with the light beyond description,
serves Spirit, the indwelling, outgoing presence ever near,
and I am so grateful I caught on fast,
only a few incarnations of muddling through the muck,
much needed for the learning and earning the difference.

What a difference a lifetime makes!
What a difference a day makes in the life of Soul!
What a difference each moment makes,
living in this garden of gratitude.

Nourished by laughter and tears,
let freedom wring me out to dry
in God's time.
About time I get it!

## I Greet the Divinity Within You

A stranger passing by on the street,
not so strange—eyes meet—hearts connect.
Recognition bursts the silence,
speaking a smile, greeting God within You.

A baby crying out its sound,
communicating, though not quite understood
until a glance of Love catches its eye,
and light fills its being.

A butterfly rides the wind,
kisses a flower to drink the sweet nectar of love,
as dew drops slip away in the morning sun.

Every living thing shines through
sowing seeds of creativity,
fertilized only when recognition of
Its true worth is realized.

Eye to eye
Heart to heart
Soul to Soul
Greeting the divinity within the miracle of life living within you in
its splendor—a touch—a whisper—a sigh

Beyond time and space
again we meet as strangers, as friends,
stilled by the silence served for dessert,
eat the sacredness fried and
seasoned by all that is holy.

Each greeting given and received quickens knowing.
Recognition sharpening our lives
by living in total awareness,
in sacred recognition,
Moment by moment
saluting the Divinity within the
pregnant-pause prayer song,
calling the listening out to dine
on the invisible.
Stuffing self with appetizers of eternity.

A chance meeting in passing
Greeting the Divinity within you
Leaving you hungry for the main course of consciousness.

"Eat drink and be merry."
Life is a banquet of loving divinity.
Dinner is served.
Will you come?

## *After Hours Musing*

Loving the enchanting energy of the midnight hour,
filling the night with softness,
announcing sweet wonders,
as Souls sail away on their dreams for the night.

I love this time for its hidden mystery
of quiet expressions,
like a soft kiss, the fullness of loving promises
held within the sanctuary of the heart.
Holding no questions and all the answers
take flight into the knowingness.

Day time, night time, anytime, no time, without time
Do you have time to feast on this silence?
Do you know love?
Do you know Love?
Can you see Love in all its glory?

Can you behold love in the eye of the beholder?
As beauty is in the eye of a needle in a hay stack
do not seek to hide behind the empty phrases,
through back door places where nothing is hidden.

For what I seek is invisible in its true form.
Perceived only in its actions demonstrated,
just so you know Love exists.
Why?
Because God is Love
and
Soul exists because of God's Love for It.

## All or Nothing at All

When blue birds sing, and whippoorwills call
and willows weep for me,
I find I am standing on holy ground,
even though at times I feel grounded,
ground up into fine fragments of stardust
being swept away by the broom
of life, or a dust mopping the debris from my life.

Which is good, so they say, whoever they are.
Sprinkled without a shaker, unmeasured filaments of
imagination filtered through the merry-go-round,
looking for merry and bright in this dark night of Soul
in delightful recognition of Its greatness.

Hey, I Am that! Yes I am.
Yet this awareness won't buy a hill of beans,
if I don't tend them with loving care,
like the tender bloom of a rose,
blossoming in silent beauty,
adorning truth begotten for a song and dance.

Laughter speaks of tales untold,
of a journey unfolding, going the distance
unlimited, finding no twilight zone,
finding always only oneself in lovely yet
lonely solitude, where love songs are sung in minor keys,
as the heart distills the melody of learning the hard way.

If only
I could listen more
If only
I could love more
If only
I could die more,
If only
I could serve more,
Then I would l have the last laugh, if there is such
a thing as the last laugh.
For of a truth, there is no such thing as a last anything,
first of all.

So here and now it is decided the songs of the heart,
sung to the Creator,
written in the key of living one's truth,
to go to the ends of the earth and beyond,
where rainbows play hide and seek
with light and darkness.

For they can be seen only after sun showers bring forth
a promise of lost stars;
mercy and love leading me blindly on and on,
as I chant repetitively to myself,
"Just keep going, don't stop."

This journey is not a lifetime journey, it's forever.
Yes, a day and night time, right time, falls through
twilight's gated entrance
into sublime understanding.

Oh yes, now I see...the fine line
Between knowledge and wisdom,
speaking and listening,

directed and non-directed prayer,
self-will, God will,
living and dying,
humility-humiliation
divinity-madness.

All the fine lines of distinctions measured
in silent moments marching across the grand divide
to arrive at the mighty moat of heaven's door,
which opens only from the inside,
and each of us as Soul, must open this door.

This is a riddle you say? Why?
Soul must knock on the door of heaven
for it to open from the inside.
I, Soul, must open this door from within,
to discover I arrived before I came
to this moment, standing still...

To passionately immerse one's self, in one's own
divinity, quickly, before the moment cracks open
and down stars fall, yet up they go, for
distance is near and far, closer than a heartbeat,
for the Presence of the Beloved prevails
as I abide within IT.

Nothing has power over the Light and Sound,
and in this sacred place all illusions and shadows
that hide are gone in this golden moment,
to stay gone forever,
if I stay in this moment of now,
each moment demands
All or nothing at All.

Oh my, it is up to me!
stay or not, there is only this moment...
this Divine loving gift from God, and the Beloved,
And Soul exists only in the present moment,
Now
Where else can Soul go
To Be Here Now?

## What is a Mystic?

Is everyone born with this God-given ability?
Well lets see:
A mystic
is One
who never loses his childlike wonder,
One who
Is a far-seeing one,
One who can look at a flower
and see far-flung galaxies,
One who knows
he knows nothing
for he has an intimate relationship
with the knower,
One who has
the practical wisdom of an uncluttered mind,
for of a truth, the heart holds on to nothing.

Perhaps the Mystic is one with an unwavering
trust in Spirit,
One who has gained true simplicity.
Perhaps the Mystic is you and me,
as we are called to remember,
to BE the Rememberer, and know
I Am That!

And with the mystical experiences
revealed within the Heart of a Mystic,
It knows it must now go beyond the mystic
into the Heart of God,

to know the unknown as it is revealed through
Divine Love and God's Grace,
to know Truth,
the whole Truth.

## *Alone With Oneself*

Listen to yourself when you are alone.
Solitude whispers in moments of quiet repose,
speaking your truth.

Those who help themselves, stand and wait.
Yet, time waits for no one, and when you are alone,
in moments out of time, tune out all of the
mindless chatter
so you can hear as you listen to the secrets of love.

Always known, yet forgotten,
as are ancient caves, and buried rivers
flowing beneath layers of crusty earth, hidden,
forbidden within the eye of newt
and eggs of dragons' breath.
And what is recorded of these words is born of empty
nothings leading to...
something is amiss, yet missed.

How to listen to yourself when alone.
Are you true to yourself when no one is listening?
No one is looking out for you in mindless games,
for to play or stay is not important.
Soul cannot leave itself in a lurch,
when seeking heaven's door before it closes,
which can never open, except with the key of love.

So it goes, and going is gone.
Left to its own devices, the light of a thousand suns
begins to shine unfettered.

Purity turns up the volume of understanding and the
wakened consciousness casts off shadows offensive in
their illusions, in vain, covering truth, for nothing lies
in words bordering on the shores of truth's learning curve,
never forgotten, once remembering is jump started.

Letting go of beaten, faded ideas no longer applicable
when one walks among the stars
listening to the cry of the hawk
and the cry in the night.

When listening to yourself when you are alone,
what is it you hear?

## Besides You, Who Cares?

What is the status of the ego gone astray?
What is it that today you take a stand and say,
enough--you may not treat me in such a rude way,
to make a point, pointless though it may be.
Because if they knew better,
you would not be having this conversation with yourself,
and worse, it gets no where.

And why does it matter? It doesn't.
So lighten your load and move along
to where the living is easy, inspired by
peaceful settings and people smiling and are
polite, and appreciate all you do.

No static interference to test the mortal coil,
whatever that is, and what would you be learning?
Not much.
No Soul-searching in the land of no-jerks-live-here
to try your patience.
Nothing to test your spiritual endurance.

If you stay, boredom will assault you,
hunt you down to the bone.
Nothing will be in your face to challenge you,
just all the smiles all the whiles the niceness
so sticky sweet, leaves you stuck in the muck
of believing this is what you want.

When did you ever want the easy way?
You are a warrior of the heart,
a champion of divine love,
and you know it don't come easy.

The hard way, the only way is to feel the slings and arrows
thoughtlessly slung, slinging you along for the ride.
Nothing is personal, don't you remember?
Nothing is about you,
so forget the whining, no excuses ever.
It is all part of the grand design to see what gets your goat,
and you don't even have a goat.
The joke is on you.

The joke is on you
if you ever fall into forgetting the first cause.
Anything else is ridiculous, hilarious.

Where did you leave your sense of humor
that you, at a moment's notice
could forget to laugh at yourself?
What a trip, tripping self up, up and away,
yet it is very clear,
God's love is here to stay.

## Brought Back

I am a child of the light and sound,
one who is brought back to now,
to give all that is, or has ever been given
to anyone who needs to know, Love is real.

Reminding all, if you think you have
reached the end of the Journey,
it has not begun until it is realized,
the closer you get to the end,
the farther away it is.
Distance is illusion.

If you think you know all you need to know,
keep learning.
If you lay your body down to sleep,
keep dreaming, but don't forget to wake up.
If you think you are too busy,
stop and smell the flowers.
If you think you are living life
to the fullest, think again.

Rather, don't think.
Stop thinking, for your journey has not yet begun,
not until you throw caution to the wind,
and take risks of the heart.
What can be more important than
remembering who and what you are?

More than, less than,
all things are contained within the cosmic sea of life,
the sacred sound HU,
instilled with the gift of wisdom.

Love leads the way to Thy kingdom come,
only Thy will be done,
or gone once again, for it is not done yet,
searching for questions you forgot to ask,
the questions you forgot the answers to.

Two for one sale, yes, waking up is hard to do.
But ask yourself, what else do you have to do?
Right, nothing?
Nothing from nothing leaves nothing,
so what is your equation?
What is your reason for being here?
Why have you been brought back?

Say thank you for the reason,
thank you, Beloved, for loving me
thank you for trusting me
thank you for the gift of consciousness
But what do you say when thank you just don't cut it?
Say thank you anyway,
God hears all the words spoken or unspoken.

Words that sing within the heart of HU.

## Growing

Growing in, growing out, growing up--
an ongoing process.
Yet in one phase of growing up,
my mother use to say to me,

"Remember, children should be seen-not heard."
No wonder I grew up wondering if anyone was listening!
A herd of elephants stalking crystal
in a china shop, wham-bam, bulls eye.

Bring it on home, kernels of Truth
so I can make a necklace
shining with wisdom, both ancient and new,
to restore my faith, my heart.

For the eternal nature of Soul is strengthened
through the comforting touch of understanding,
which releases all impediments to
the free flow of wisdom,
creaking its way back to square one,
in the beginning, yet never ending saga,
of getting rid of all the baggage of misconceptions
dimming the light of Soul.
Did you pay your Light bill?

Nothing is ever wasted or lost in the stars,
when the key of creativity is found--
Soul's birthright, to create Its
Masterpiece for living in concert,

co-creating its true reality, freed from the
Illusion that you are the center of the universe.

God is love. It lives within true simplicity of
the heart, (in small things) with great love.
No labor lost,
no song unsung,
no poem unheard,
no sincere prayer unanswered,
and why?

Whatever appears lost, reappears found,
so let go.
Remember God's will be done.
Surrender to your heart and if you listen,
all you will ever need to know, you will.

So delight in the Garden of your Divinity which
you plowed with blood sweat and tears.
I trust the discipline of love
survived the journey,
so put all the learning to work
in Spiritual endeavors, serving all Life.

No fears, many tears, to nourish Soul,
growing through being the Song of HU.
Be life's greatest student--
a Spiritual Giant is born, a masterpiece
yet to be finished.

The learning and growing polishes Soul,
and through this continual process
of Soul's education, grace and gratitude
transform this, and all lifetimes into

being what it Is--
A Great Adventure!

And as a Wise Man I met on this journey, once said
"Remember, you can't make a flower grow by pulling it."

## Can It Get Any Better Than This?

The sound of breaking glass,
or the sound of a breaking heart,
or the sound of giving all that one has to give,
for I know only the heart can cry the tears of Soul.

Yet, the fragments remain as reminders that
what is broken can come together, but
the cracks that are mended by the glue of life,
tell silent stories of the breaking of form.

And what is form? It is a holding container
for the substances of the living waters of Holy Spirit,
but beyond form.
It is what is hidden from a heart seeking to understand,
and cries out for answers,
yet, when answers come, they seem meaningless.

As a spiritual quest, consider:
Soul is contained in the body,
the acorn contains the oak tree,
yet, beyond all form, there is the formless.

When grasping the great form without form,
Soul knows true freedom.
It is this essence that holds the secret of transformation.

Spiritual directions accompany Soul in all its journeys,
no matter the direction.

The true north of God Will,
will always lead Soul into the heart of the matter,
for all that matters is the Heart of God.

No way is there to go, which will not take you where
you need to be in each and every moment,
if you listen, if you listen,
if you listen,
and wait.
Wait for the inner direction before acting, and why?
For one simple reason: do I act alone, all on my own?
No, I await the inner direction before acting.
I am not a free agent,
but an agent of the Divine plan.

I don't know what this is in total, yet I trust totally,
with absolute reliance, wherever the moment leads me,
wherever Spirit needs me,
I know I will be there, I know I will follow.

There were times when I acted on my own,
and a mess did I make.
It took me lifetimes to clean it up.

So with this knowing, it is easy to surrender
my will, my all,
to The Beloved, the one who teaches me
the ways of gentleness.
The one who gives me eyes to see and hear,
the biting call to serve,
the one who gives me all that I need
to be of loving service to all life.

If I need patience, the lesson is there again,

as long as it takes.
If I need trust, or more Divine love, it is there,
all I need and more.
Through true contemplation of the
never-ending study of spiritual consciousness,
I keep my eternal appointment with the Beloved.

Always with me,
Never leaving me, ever, I am never alone.
How wonderful to walk the walk side by side
inside outside
With the Beloved.
So the question is, what is real for you?
What could possibly be the difficulty?
Do you trust and believe in God?
And when sleep won't come, do you wonder,
why is this life we are living so hard?
May I ask you to consider,
what is stronger than the Light and Sound of God?
What can assail Divine Love within Its fortress
Of God's Grace?

Nothing has power over Truth,
and only fear can remove Soul
from this place where love lives forever.
Let go the illusions that tear you apart.

If your heart must break in order to know God,
Let it break, break wide open, without a doubt.
If your heart must break, let it be for a noble cause,
Not for sniveling fear.
Love must enter the heart without limitations.

How awesome are the spiritual gifts given Soul

this lifetime, to use, to apply, to plant, to harvest,
to increase Soul's spiritual capacity to love.
And somehow through all the hardships,
we find compassion has come to stay in the Heart.

To give love like you have never given before,
to live in Spirit like you have never lived before,
to know until this moment, you were never so alive
as when you are embraced in the loving arms of Spirit.

No more doubts, no more fears,
now you know
God Loves Me?
God Loves Me!

Yes, Soul exists because of God's Love.
All would perish without this love.
It just is. It is a given.

When Soul awakens to this reality,
all things change.
Soul is baptized in the living waters of Holy Spirit.
Can it get any better than this?

## Dream Teachings

Little did I know what awaited me last night
when Now I lay me down to sleep, most likely to dream.
However, what I experienced last night was more,
more than just a dream, yes more than a dream.

More than a dream from the ancient days,
Beyond imagination.
Why is this so? What was different last night?

This experience was unlike any that I had
experienced before--
I attended a class being presented by the great
Poet of Divine Language, Rumi!
It was thrilling! Beyond enlightening!

As I listened, what was being caught by my heart,
set my heart on fire, holding a steady flame,
as the words spoken blended all opposites into
the Divine Polarity of ONE.

How so, you may wonder?
Well it seemed I awakened often,
to write down notes to myself, tucking them into my
heart, so I would not lose them.
The words held the high vibration of the
Spiritual Language of Soul.
I recorded them, as best as I could, and returned to class.

When I awoke the next morning, I could barely read
what I had written.
These are some of the fragments I brought back from this adventure:

*Do you not see what lies are hidden beneath*
*the pyramids, still sleeping in consciousness,*
*to yet awaken to ancient mysteries.*
*Now dreams and certainty escape your lips,*
*slipping unseen into your heart.*

*As dawn caresses you*
*with painful awareness, it rips aside veils*
*of sorrow's lament,*
*Where are you Beloved one?*

*In the missing of you, Beloved,*
*tears cascade down my cheeks,*
*falling upon the dust of centuries waiting*
*for your return.*

*I sweep away the residue left behind*
*from the ancient of days.*
*Listening to these conversations within the deepest*
*part of me waits for*
*no answer, answering itself~*
*within the worlds of Love, Light and Sound,*
*where even a whisper cries aloud,*
*breaking open the door of Soul,*
*crushing Life and Living into Being True.*

*Souls do not sleep in this place,*
*Where even dreams slumber.*
*Forgetfulness not an option,*
*NO, wake up in the blink of an eye or*
*All may be forgotten.*

*How could you forget love? Love in its entirety,*
*that has been eating your heart out of its*
*resting place, now rise into action and clean your temple.*
*Then you will not feel like your longing for God*
*is akin to dying.*

*At the altar of forgotten songs begotten for your sake,*
*so stay awake,*
*Child of the Light and Sound.*

*Feel the presence of the Living One*
*Breathe its living breath into your being.*
*Feel The Beloved touch your brow,*
*this sets your very molecules vibrating,*
*thrusting you, Dear Soul, into sheer ecstasy,*
*knowing you have learned and earned the deepest secret...*
*How to receive the blessings of eternity.*

## Truth in Celebration

Moving through the jungle of life,
footsteps sounding like a herd of
elephants, no subtlety there, or here,
why do I provoke thought?

Only when thoughtless waves
assault the senses, no defense for
there is none.
It is always a choice
to keep the blinders on,
shielding you from truth. Why?
Truth is too painful.

The lie—deceptive in its promise of comfort--
yet there will come a moment when you are out of time.
In that moment, the state of grace emerges.
Holding forth the mirror of Soul,
it waits for each Soul to come face to face
with Its Truth, Its Heart song.

And when we turn away in the Spirit of
abandonment, not a pretty sight,
it is the stuff of nightmares
and the cry in the night.

Yet nothing is ever lost, for
the womb of darkness encircles the
heart, giving birth to all of your truth,
nothing but the truth.

Pop goes the weasel round and round.
Somewhere the illumination of courage
purifies the heartfelt truth, be told.

Divine turning point of Grace, as a beacon,
a shining example of Soul unfettered.

## Certain in Uncertainty

There was a time in the world of certainty where
all uncertainty dwelled, and it did not matter for sure,
for the answers did not come with questions.
The whys and why nots were
not a big thing, for one thing was certain:

From the very heart of God,
this never-ending quest compels Soul to
never give up.
Even in the face of the end,
keep going past the end.

And if you think you have found the answers,
look again.
One can never see it all, for
all keeps changing, forever in motion,
blending, bending, sending vibrations
far and near, never fear, love is here.

And for certain there is no final curtain,
as a matter of fact there is no finality,
or curtain, or certainty, and nothing is lost
forever in its finding itself, only to discover.

What is found has nothing to do with
staying the course, beyond known and unknown.
Remembered, yet forgotten dreams take flight,
flown the coop, they could not stay awake.
Embraced in the arms of slumber, overtakes
mistakes.

It is just one of all the ways into understanding the
outstanding debt gratitude pays for the opening heart,
is everything it is cracked up to be, and not to be
makes little difference in God's plan for Soul.

Selfless surrender washes all that is preshrunk,
no more to shrink when hanging out to dry,
wet and soaked in platitudes.
Enough already, of this I am certain.

I want real, raw, and shredded in the grinder
of living...whatever it is
The toll road is the high road, and whatever toll it takes,
take it all, take it all or nothing at all,
of this I am certain, until I breathe the last
breath within this mortal coil...and inhale
Life in the heavenly worlds.

I Am the least of servants of the Beloved

## *If You Don't Want, You Don't Have To*

Have ever you wondered, "How did I get here?"
Answers may vary, yet
basically the experience in consciousness,
even though a variable,
is always the same.

If you are in a place you do not want to be,
it does not matter how you got here or there,
or why, or if you question yourself --
"What was I thinking?" (or not thinking.)
The answers are questionable at best, (or worst),
so where does this moment leave you?

There is the clue:
Where did this moment leave you?
Wherever it is, it is the journey,
not the destination
which can be changed in a moment's notice!

Yes, rather than the moment leaving you,
you can leave the moment!
How about that concept?
You are the choice maker.
Your life and how you live it are expressions
of your state of consciousness,
and we have all heard,
"A miracle is a changed consciousness."

Choice is sacred; change is sacred,

Life is sacred.

Each moment you spend, each moment you breathe,
what you exhale leaves an imprint
within the fabric of life.
So when you find yourself
where you don't want to be,
Be somewhere else; there is nothing stopping you.

The only requirement is,
wherever you are, BE what you are,
walking on Holy Ground
in full awakened consciousness,
taking responsibility for you.

Be the Love that you are.
Live in this Love you magnify
to the worlds of God and Man,
then it matters not where you are.

Just don't forget to breathe what you are,
for when you put the power of Soul
into every action, thought, and deed,
it tells all who come into your presence
who and what you are.
It tells the condition of your heart.

Recognize and accept your Divinity.
Embrace the God-like qualities within you
and you will see this reflected back at you.

So don't fret, just Be.
Rest in the awareness that you, me, everyone,
are the Children of the Creator.

We hold high the sacred flame
of Love, Wisdom, Freedom,
but most of all, Love,
so others can find their way.

And lest we forget, we are here to serve all life,
in all circumstances,
in this testing ground of Soul.

## Changes

Is any day just like any other day?
Of course not, silly goose.
Not one moment is like any other
for the simple reason there is no reason or season, seasoning life
with enticing appetite.

Beauty wields a sword with great dignity and honor,
As a Celtic song of longing for freedom
ringing in the ears of forever.

Yet, never to know the why of Allness,
this love of not mine or yours, is not owned
but given, and the ways of Heart Knowing
superseding all things bright and beautiful,
giving them life among the stars,
while cosmic winds blow away patterns,
rising above and away, staying in the path of love.

In truth, what truth, what is the way to know?
Truth be told, behold only through experience.
Recognition blasts away concrete abstracts
that may come close, for experience is naught
unless the experiment brings transformation,
leaving one changed forever...if remembered.

What is it I seek? To live in consciousness of Truth,
not just in practice, but as a living reality.
This golden glistening wisdom that I swallow,
digest and distill in stillness in the still of the night,

and sleep? No time for sleep.
For that matter, no time for time.

I choose to be living truth.
The proof that it is what I am, and I am that truth within
the stronghold of love- The Temple within.

## It Is My Desire

No matter how Soul gets here it got here just the same,
tattered and torn, weary and worn, down and out,
for the journey is long.
Sometimes the pain is longer,
yet, no longer a point of attention.

Along the way... the wonder of living and dying,
learning how to give and receive Divine Love,
letting go in finding the path of least resistance,
knowing I have nothing to prove and nothing to lose,
for all things gravitate to me
in the Spirit of Service.
I rest in the heart of contentment.

Even though the slings and arrows
of daily living assault and batter me,
I will not be detained in this glorious
journey that is not for the faint-hearted.

The Way is the testing ground
for Souls who want Mastership,
Only... to be of greater service to all life,
demonstrating God's Love for Soul,
and wherever Spirit needs me
in service to Life.
That's where I want to be.

And though deep within,
there is joy beyond description,

there are times
when my cries of despair can be heard
throughout the Heavens, and my tears
become the floodgate of Soul, as worlds
turn upside down colliding with agendas
and plans and goals held tightly,
though rightly the planning may be.
Flexibility is the way of least resistance.

Consider this: Change comes.
The fluidity of consciousness
cleans the slate and opens new vistas
beyond our imagination
and beyond our wildest dreams.
I believe it is Divine will in action,
always making room for Soul's growth.

And what a beautiful sight, Soul facing
the unknown fearlessly knowing what may
come, or go, yet with courage, faces timeless
Truth, for Soul has learned not to take itself seriously.

So it laughs and sings to the high
heavens with gratitude, that it is only by Grace
that It is worthy to take up sword and shield
defending what needs no defense,
in the name of Love, by all that is Holy,
stands its ground, no backing down,
no matter whatever, for Soul knows only
to love and serve the Beloved is reason for Its
living
being
giving
loving
breathing.

What a blessing,
what a lifetime,
what a holy mess I am at times,
and yet the compassion and care
the Beloved bestows on me, Soul,
is priceless,
and I withhold nothing from You ever,
and I stand before You clothed in naked truth,
and You see me,
a beautiful shining Soul.

And so, Beloved One, my one desire is to reflect
your glory and love to all, as it flows through me
unchanged to touch all that I meet...
This is my desire.

# Crucible of The Heart

What beauty is born in the crucible of the heart?
Those moments of despair that seem to crunch the
very life out of me, yet in their wake, leave golden
blessings, fragile in their being, singing
with grace and purity, knowing the way into
the presence of God, comes always with great sacrifice.

Yet Soul cares nothing for the cost; it gladly pays
the bill for services rendered, surrendering all
to fulfill the requirements demanded of Soul.

Moving closer to God,
the heights, the depths, the all encompassing
presence that kisses the heart, the painful
touch scars the tender heart with its searing
love, and no matter what comes, Soul cries out,

"Whatever it takes, take it all, leave nothing of me,
for I am nothing without Spirit breathing life into me.
I am undone, I am ecstatic,
for contentment fills me with nothing left to lose."

Lost is a place I found
long ago and far away, in silent dreams between
lifetimes spent at the edge of eternity
with longing so deep the pain seemed more
than Soul could bear, yet somehow I did survive,
sometimes it seemed, barely hanging by a thread.

Then a brief remembrance would stir deep inside,
an awakening, yes, a land of golden, silent secrets
whispering light and sound, calling Soul to
catch the gift waves, to ride into the light
shining beyond the borders of heaven.

So when forces combine to batter me,
I am strong, in my weakness, I go down on bended knees,
yet I do not waver in this testing, this challenge to
stay on the razor's edge of consciousness,
for it is life itself
and I dare to immerse myself in Love forever.

At times the tests are so hard they wring the
tears out of my heart, rending an anguished cry,
Help me God, Help me...I can't do this on my own.

Only Holy Spirit moves me in ways
unknown, yet with complete trust I am moved
by the wind from the mountain of God,
surrendered, unresisting the battering ram,
so when times come to stretch me thin,

I am gentled by an accepting heart, born to
love all life, no matter what.

I came back this lifetime to earn Mastership,
no pussy footing around, no wimping out.
I embrace the crucible of the heart
as I become a greater student of Life
step by step, moment by moment,

For the ways of Spirit are ancient, yet
new to me, forever easy to remember,

so hard forgetting.
Beauty speaks its creative likeness into
Soul desiring nothing, just to love and honor
its Truth, with effortless effort, for it just is.

Soul, just IS the seed
planted in the heart, taking root
with conscious awareness of Its Divinity.
For Soul to give all that it has to give, and then, more,
practicing the discipline of Love.

Strengthening Soul's capacity to meet the
ever increasing demands Spirit makes of Soul
in the moment,
this is all there is,
for the moment is now and now
is the eternal nature of Soul.

I am joyful and grateful for all opportunities given me,
to make great or small offerings, to say thank you
with love to Spirit for this precious lifetime of service.

## Dear God, Let Me Serve Thee

You are the worlds beyond description, the worlds
unseen, yet ever near, ever present,
Holy Sound that ignites my days and nights,
calling me forth to your Presence ever more,
and more and more, you reveal more of the All
that is you.

I have known you forever in the
Presence and the Essence of
The Beloved One,
Your gift of Love to Soul,
to all Souls, awakens the heart song of HU.

All that I am, is because you love me,
and today as always, I find myself in your Presence,
as scales fall from the blinded eye.
Now I can see your glory and blessings
in all things.
Within all, your love is here,
there, everywhere there is a wherever.

And so I ask, as always, just let me be
of greater service.
And you, as always, say to my heart
"It is done." So do.

Do all in the name of the Beloved,
and I do so dearly rejoice in all the ways
You bless me to serve You, in all life,
all living, all love.

A smile, a helping hand, a listening heart,
a crust of bread and such, and such is Your
greatness, you give me your All, so
I may give this All of You to all life.

You give me Love unconditionally,
so I may give this unconditional love to all life.
You give me strength, understanding, joy, sorrow,
all of your unlimited resources
to fulfill every task you ask of me.
You give me the grace of experience, so I may know the
greatness of Soul, and recognize my own Divinity.

In this sacred surrendering, in this moment,
you withhold nothing, for each moment is a gift
for giving to whatever Spirit needs of me.

God listens to the cry in the night,
hearing the beseeching prayer of a Soul asking for a sign,
a sign, just to let It know,
It is not lost,
It is not alone,
even when Soul may forget who It is, or
that God Loves It.

God does not forget ever. *Every Soul matters.*

The gifts of God go forth from awakened loving hearts,
the servants of the ONE servant,
those dedicated in Its service, to be in the right place
in each moment, to be the smile, the answered prayer.

And lest I forget, dear God, I remember, always,
when I heard the cry in the night, and you opened

the floodgates of my listening heart, and I could hear
the cry of every Soul in Its longing for God,
and lo and behold, my cry was the loudest of them all.

Yes, I am free to love thee in the deepest purity
of my heart of hearts.
Yes, I am forever grateful you trust me
to serve you in all ways,
and the truth of your Living Essence abides within me.
So again I say,
just let me be of greater Service to thee.

And when the time comes to leave this mortal coil,
the only change will be the way this Soul will
continue in your service.

Forever.
For you are Love, I am Love
and love is Always,
Always Love
Thank you.

## Just Wondering

Just wondering,
How does one continue serving when
Soul moves on after this physical body gives out?

From what little I have seen, what little I remember,
there is freedom, real freedom.
There is joy that is boundless.
And the Love, leaves me breathless.

But who needs to breath
when the physical body gives out?
All is Love,
Love is All.

There is reunion with other Souls who made the journey
beyond the borders of death before me.
And the service continues.
What is it like, I wonder,
without these physical laws that are so adverse to Soul's
desire to serve God, to love all life,
to be the fulfillment of the dream God dreams for us
as Soul.

Not to know ourselves, as much as it is
to learn who we are.
And in loving ourselves, love God.
To know God,
even with this returning wave of living and dying,
even with this discovery, we know nothing.

With all the learning,
With all the growing,
With all the loving,
With all the letting go,
With all the moving beyond restrictions,
With embracing no limitations
With all the ifs, ands, and buts
The if only,
The cries in the night, the despair, the loneliness,
The dark night of Soul
Is but a split second at the edge of eternity,
and dark side of moonless shadows,

Causing the clinging to shreds of evidence that proclaim
yes, there is life after life
death after death,
living and dying,
Yes, within and without all the memories,
Without all the experiences of lifetimes of learning,
What is the delight of Soul's Journey
Into all the tomorrows, and the days after whatever,
All this is designed to shape something out of nothing
Which we do all the time anyway,
making do, doing without.

There are worse things than hunger.
Would you dare say this to one whose belly
is distended from malnutrition?
What on earth would
cause someone dying of starvation to believe this?

And on the next rerun, this Soul remembers
that lifetime experience
and vows to never go hungry again.

Not on your life, any life,
And this is the way of life and living here and there.

Only until one knows the true hunger
of Soul's longing for God,
the Spiritual calories that bring sustenance,
The lightening sound crashing through all barriers
like a tornado of cosmic proportions
blown outward like constellations giving birth
to galaxies across space
Starlight star bright
May I have this wish I wish tonight?

Tonight, foolish one? What about the rest of eternity?
What about now, or then
Or when or where?
It all is summed up in the eye of a needle
Or dust in the eye of Love.

The spinning continues everywhere at once
And for comprehension we think this is only playing
Out here...hear ye, hear ye.

Yet it is all one big fat crescendo!
The finale of a silent symphony--
One sound
One note
One voice
One cry
One heartbeat
It
Is
Just
LOVE
just wondering.

## Finding Ourselves in God's Grace

We drink confusion,
we breath illusion.
We trip and fall over delusion,
and when there is doubt, let it out
without a doubt, for whatever the reason
that blindness sets in, the only way out is to open
the heart, and let the mind go out to play.

Stay out of the way of Spiritual endeavors seeking
ways to the worlds of Spirit turned upside down,
even though trouble is a challenge to sanity.

The overcoming of all things is love,
purity of heart, sincerity of heart—
A good place to start moving into the
returning journey home again.

The only treasure to rely on is the currency of love.
A surrendered mind is a true servant,
subservient to Spirit.
Purification begins in Soul's quest
into the sea of remembrance,
re-acquainting self with truths known from other times,
forgotten in other times.

The journey is long, and the way into direct knowing
has many pitfalls designed to let go the belief in opposites.

For it is this belief that sets up roadblocks and detour signs,
lending to the confusion, brought about by illusion,
as cunning as Wiley Coyote in his pursuit of Road Runner,
whose character reflects the trusting Spirit
of one who believes in himself, and the goodness
of the universe as a causative agent.
If one thinks they are confused, the clue is think.

The mind thinks it is confused.
If one confuses illusion with reality, consider the source.

Where oh where is the sense in this senseless world
in which we find ourselves?
I know, an alien land, not our true home,
and the only GPS: the Spiritual Exercises,
the lifeline of Soul
in the sparkling lands of Holy Spirit.

The only refuge for Soul, beyond the grasp of the mind,
mindless in its pursuit of sowing seeds of doubt,
is for Soul to sow seeds of gratitude and appreciation,
and a loving heart dedicated to serving the Beloved.
Can we not open the eye of Soul and see beyond
the next Dunkin' Donuts©, the blessings of Spirit
embracing us with God's Grace?

Spiritual liberation is not a fantasy.
This earth world is not just fantasy,
it is an addiction for the mind's playground,
and there are many clever dead-ends,
unless we see with the eyes of Soul,
high above this earthly world
where the light and sound of God casts no shadows,
has no echoes, just overtones

forever expanding outward within the resonating
vibrations of all sounds, all life, all living,
all hearts beating,
every note breathing the sound of a flute
strong and pure in the listener's heart.
Behold...hear...the music of God.

The silent hush between the inflow and outflow of the
Divine breath
is where all things not of Itself, are erased
through the process of purification come clean.

Let the Spiritual scrubbing bubbles do their work
so Soul breathes the air of service,
and the polluted atmosphere of this earth world
does not deter the Spiritual determination
of Soul on its mission,
its returning journey into the heart of God.

The polluting agents of anger, greed, vanity,
attachment and lust...
are as popcorn popping in the kettle of illusion
in the movie house of Spiritual deception,
where no longer is there a hold on Soul.

All the efforts are puny,
for Soul lost the taste to drink confusion,
or breathe illusion.

Soul inhales Holy Spirit
and exhales Its love for Soul;
knowing without a doubt the only true reality is
Soul's relationship with God.

And as another character wisely said,
"Th-th-th-that's that's all folks...."
all the rest is loony tunes.

The end.

## The Universal Lost and Found

In this world of extraordinary people
living ordinary lives, it occurs to me, that the state
of lostness must be qualified by place.
For instance, if one is lost, most times this is followed
by a where.

Lost in the wilderness
Lost in the jungle
Lost in my mind
Lost at sea
Lost in despair
Lost in love
Lost in the stars
Lost my way
Lost, lost, lost, where oh where am I lost?

Does it matter, do you care?
Being lost is good for me,
because when I lose my way and
the surroundings are familiar,
I can say, oh yeah, I know where I am,
I was lost here before,
and now I know my way to where I am going,
I may not know where I am going, but I am not lost.

Enough senseless chatter,
this world is spinning out of control!
Each night the moon changes position in the night sky.
The chaos and stress on the psyche of man
is extreme to say the least, more or less.

To share this planet with every other living
entity requires some kind of insanity.
Consider, the planet itself is bipolar,
and no Xanax© for mother earth.
Put upon by its inhabitants, who without mercy
Show no respect for the resources of this earth.

Yet survival of all life depends on cultivating good will,
our restoring harmony, balance, reverence, gratitude
for all we receive that sustains us, keeps us found,
and where does it start?
Within the heart of man.
The healing force for this planet and for all life
is the HU.

We must become the HU,
No more time to talk about this.

Get off our high horse, or get on and ride,
ride like the wind carrying this love song
to the four corners of this planet.

The storm song of cloud formations softly echo the song,
and the sun bathes us in its light,
so we can see the coming of the new spiritual day,
after Soul's journey through a long spiritual night,
to earn spiritual maturity.

Fear has outdistanced itself,
and love stands alone on the pinnacle
of God's holy, life-saving grace.
Without God's love all life would perish.

What would that be like?
Can we even imagine no love, no life, before
it all began, before there was anything?
Go back to where it all began,
before anything was?

Yet even in that moment, that spark,
that unit of awareness exists.
Soul is non-perishable in the beginning, in this now,
Soul exists because of God's love.

For Soul, without this, all would perish,
animate and inanimate.
Yet no matter where Soul goes,
into the deepest reaches of eternity,
God is.
Soul is.
All is this love, until the end of time.

Tit for tat, tattered robes we wear,
yet glorious refinement awaits our
acceptance of truth, that we are inheritors of the throne.

Back to lost...
Claim your liberty, use it or lose it, be free,
it is never too late, so the story goes,
and good stories are never lost
on the collective consciousness of man.

For hidden in the deepest recess,
memory stirs beneath the surface,
recalling Soul moments of learning love, giving love.

The heart awakens to all the blessings
on the playing field of life, while this planet--
Mother Earth, keeps on spinning round and round
calling forth harmony of the galaxies and
constellations spinning,
gravity keeping all in order and place, controlling chaos.
With millions upon millions of atoms,
singing cosmic renderings of
All that is, was and ever will be, all is not lost.

As night falls, crickets sing.
Here comes the morning dew
like tear drops dressing flowered petals,
holding the reflection
of the morning light.

## *The View From Within*

To clearly see what needs to be seen
for visionary insight, looking within to see
what is required when the tests come
through the Five Virtues.
Yes, Humility, Detachment, Discrimination,
Tolerance/Forgiveness and Contentment.

When one travels the high road,
no longer are the opposites pulling away
from the center, centered in Spirit all day
and night, the blast of wind from the mountain
of God keeps the attention on the Sacred Sound,
HU, as it whispers a silent refrain.

For survival, Soul must serve the Great Servant.
To develop balance in all Spiritual endeavors
Soul must use the gifts given by Spirit,
for the upliftment of all beings, all life.

The unfoldment of Soul must bring
Spiritual maturity, it must walk the path of Love
with confidence, and above all else, self honesty,
for this brings humility to Soul, strengthening
It to withstand, beyond all understanding,
the true reality, where one gains the gift
to receive in full measure, God's Love.

And with Gratitude, you recognize you have
been given all, yes, all the gifts of Spirit

the Master gave you/Soul eons ago,
when the world was young and Soul
was learning how to accept the gifts of Spirit.
The Beloved held nothing back.

Trust entered the picture, absolute trust and reliance
on the Beloved Master, whose trust in me, Soul,
is beyond measure, opening the Heart,
to the eternal rhythm of Spirit.

Discovering the letters that compose words,
the notes that compose melodies,
the beat of time, timelessly sings the song of
the Great Law, Do all with Love and you will find
the Love Divine.
This is the only way.

The view from the Heart is all that matters,
seeing beauty from the inside out.
To behold joy, unfettered, free from judgments,
suppositions, impositions that no longer gain entry
into the consciousness of Soul, for they pass
like storm clouds and gray skies on the
ever changing horizon.

When Trust is absolute,
Soul knows the Sun's gonna shine,
the moon is going to rise, just as sure as
stars shining bright above, lead to the
knowing of the presence of indwelling Spirit.

The deepest longings take flight into
a renewing moment out of time,
timeless, ageless, down through the ages,

experiences written and recorded
within the book of the Heart,
telling the story of one Soul rising,
and the endless, never-ending journey,
brings Soul to the eye of the needle.

To enter through the eye of the needle,
what is there to say?
what is there to do?
Keep my heart out of dead lock,
for I have claimed my Spiritual inheritance
to the kingdom of heaven,
where foreclosures do not exist,
the only fore is foregone in conclusion
to live within the consciousness
of the basic fundamentals of Spirit.

This is my daily bread, nourishment for Soul.
I have learned to cherish Now, and celebrate
the comings and goings of Soul through
the portals of Life and Death.

For each moment dies, birthing a new Now,
throughout eternity, where the eye of the needle waits,
for weary travelers prepared to enter.

Yet to enter, Soul must give up everything--
Every gift, talent, heart-knowing certainty,
even the basic fundamental beliefs that have
carried Soul thus far. Drop it all!
Even what you think you know.
All thought must be left behind, all longing,
there is no room.

The eye of the needle requires threadbare,
bare to the bones Soul, surrendered, needing nothing.
Life and Death blend into one
glorious moment, knowing the greatest
thing Soul will ever learn
is just to give and receive divine love.

The Divine Mystery revealed after going
through the eye of the needle,
is that every surrendered talent, or gift,
Soul willingly gave up to enter this eye,
Soul finds waiting on the other side.

Now the gifts of Spirit truly belong to Soul
to use in service, to all life.
For in this challenge, it is found
all one needs is Love,
Yes!
Divine Love is the only way
through the eye of the needle.
The only way.

## Falling Tears

In songs of love it has been said
"Many a tear has to fall"
Referring to the "game" of love.

May I say, Love is not a game,
Life is not a game.
A game, so called, is not a game

No, no, stop and realize just how much you
are *not* running the show.
Are you blown about by every stray
wind, beyond your knowing?

Or do you ride the currents high above
This earthly world like noble birds?
And don't forget the eagle-eyed Adepts,
Far-seeing ones in the worlds of God.

What is it, or what makes a difference
In your movement through this universe?
Is it the call of Spirit, calling Soul home?
Or the call of your belly jellied inside?

In your pride, you go here and there thinking
you are in the driver's seat, when you are flat out
beside yourself unsurrendered
without the wonder of what to surrender,
and give up nothing.

Yet what is the surrendered state?
What is surrendered?
How about all of me, you, all of us.

# I Am Just a Fool for God

Being the true story of my experience of the living word
In the expression of living itself.
It is the transformational power
that comes like thunder and lightening.

The assault tears away everything,
And Heaven help me if there is even a shred of ego
left within there somewhere.
It must be eliminated, become non-existent for
survival of Spirit within me,
to serve from the selfless state.
All God qualities stand alone in
the worlds of no opposite.
Why is this?

The Law of Opposites dissolves
through distraction, changing attractions
by fixing attention on Love.

These worlds of duality blend into one, for
nothing has power over the Light and Sound.
No form informing, no demands to conform,
only by Law of Divine Polarity,
do all things integrate into one and the same, equal,
no division, subtraction or reaction.

In addition to Truth's living expression,
which batters me senseless because
It makes no sense to view anything with just two eyes—
when one can see with the eye of Soul.

Threadbare barely making ends meet,
in hallowed halls, through corridors
of no time for impurities, fading,
as all things gravitate to me,
no longer going out, nowhere to go,
cease striving to attain that which is unattainable.

Soul has it all.
I am alive in the Now, yes.
Soul always lives in the high worlds of Divine Spirit.
I get it, I get it.

Here I stay, while truth be told, it got me in the worlds
of Spirit's playground face to face, eye to eye, heart to heart
as the portal opens, revealing all that is.

Yes I see by God's early light, star spangled delight,
Soul liberated from all,
nothing left except a capacity to
give love, the golden coin,
ahhh, the currency of Heavenly worlds,
and with love a loving heart,
the time is come....the time is Now
Blast off---
There is an avalanche on the Mountain of God

## From the Frying Pan into the Fire

Idiotic choices,
survived through the grace of God...
the looney bin--been there done that,
those cartoon illusions keep me entertained
beyond belief, and yet my life is filled with
the ridiculous to the sublime.

knowing I can turn on a dime
I hear the high road calling my name,
yet the insanity of life keeps me busy
trying to remember what lies
forgotten in the cracks and crevices
of tomorrow may never come.

For all we do not know,
for of a fact, I know nothing at all
for all time, and here comes illusion
knocking at my door, saying
"Let me entertain you."

And Soul says, "Not on my life,
go away, you're not even real."
This much I know from lifetimes
on the funny farm, not so funny..

I died laughing a lifetime away.
O mind, how many lifetimes have you run the show?
Setting the stage designed
for Fear and Power to act out the five passions

of your mindless endeavors in pursuit of
unhappiness and pain, until it finally sinks in.
Souls rises, an awakened consciousness
and says "You can't fool me this time around,"
and around Soul goes inbound from
the edge of eternity, a Spiritual refugee
from the fields of mental exhaustion,
all the cards played out, no more games,
Soul rises triumphant, rescued by a love for all life.

As a grateful Soul, I realized early on if there is
such a thing as a Spiritual talent–
I did not have much to offer,
But I could love unconditionally...

so with this little seed in my heart growing
a great thirst for God, Soul drank deeply
of the living waters, drowning out all things
not of love ~

All illusions died of their own accord,
and a Spiritual Being
staggers from the ashes of Ego.
Soul survived countless lifetimes
of complete idiocy,
thankful God loves fools and idiots.

Yet during my tenure with illusion,
I became a fool for Love,
and found myself walking a path
where angels fear to tread.

Finally, finally,
mercy and love fueled the wasteland

of the heart, setting me, Soul, free,

granting me one request Spirit would fulfill.

All I could ask for was, let me be
of greater service
forever.

## Gaining Strength to Break Free of the Mind

Having or being, going or coming, living or dying
laughing or crying, keeping or giving away,
feet first, head first, heart tried and true comes first.

Once you allow second guessing to pause the beat,
and the blues get you down rather than make you dance,
as you seek the path of least resistance,
where all illusion tries to hide,
to blind you with its trickery, until you ask,
from what is there to hide?

So it is said,
nothing is hidden from the eye of the Tiger.
Or it all comes out in the wash and
don't throw the baby out with the bathwater,
for all things come clean eventually, in the event of
wake-up calls that crack open the mind.

The illusive wind of consciousness blows so softly,
the need of the attention fully awake and accounted for
must stand in watchful, loving understanding to hear
the message of how God speaks to us each moment,
holding forth the gift of learning and knowing
and growing.

For Soul to know that its direction into truths' way
is to always find higher ground,
for the lay of the landscape is ever changing,
so to know Truth,

for it too is ever changing.
For the same truth comes in ever new forms,
stretching the boundaries of no limitations,
into present moment's revelations,
which give pause
for Spirit to inspire imagination to bring truth
to the next level of refinement.
And it never ends.

It begins again and again, over and over, sometimes overwhelming,
sometimes overlooked, and one is caught hook, line and sinker,
until the full meaning sinks into recognition,
the image and likeness change form and reform,
giving information anew,
yet not so new, if attention stays true,
and how,
by seeing all things, all things through
Love, keeps it real,
keeps it true...for love is, all else is illusion.

Only Love has the power to make things new,
to bring the depth of certainty to the ordinary moments,
so they can be seen and caught and accepted,
as those extraordinary moments when
Truth kissed the heart,
and filled it with the true treasures of Holy Spirit.

## *I Am Here*

In answering a call to Service,
as Soul, who has earned the right to be
"First responder," I came.

I found myself in a place filled with contradictions,
warm and loving, cold and bare.
Yet love, and love alone guided my way.

From all the painful lessons earned, that was
required for me to learn, so I could
know the difference between all the opposites
that rule these worlds of duality,
just in case I had forgotten, for
how else could I be effective in service,
if I was moved by praise or criticism,
joy or sorrow, for these are the testing
means of how Soul determines what is
important, what is real, what is not,
for all of it makes little difference.

It is all the same, depending on how the
cookie crumbles, so to speak,
and learning compassion means going through
every heart-breaking and joyful experience
known to man,
and the heart finds itself in the deadlock of anguish,
yet joyful anticipation.

And I wonder, am I Soul, learning, learning, anything,
as it wrings itself out of the way.

And I know I am not here for recognition,
fame or fortune, success or failure
I am here only to serve
among the human race, forever.

And if for a moment I forget, that anything
truly matters, except for Love,
for all else is illusion, which clouds purity of heart.
But once the cobwebs are wiped away,
as Soul, I can see the deliberate design to keep me from
knowing who and what I truly am--
a child in the Wilderness of Love and Mercy,
who has been called forth, for what is beyond
rhyme or reason.

And for this privilege to be called to serve you,
to stand beside you, I will endure all things.

Your love for all Souls inspires me
To live in accord to the best of my ability,
to serve also as a lover of Souls,
in following your guidance, to somehow be of service to
those who struggle greatly to free themselves from
the snares that bring a despair, so deep,
it keeps them from clearing away the chains
of illusion that bind them, so they too can stand free.

I know, I have come through the thick and thin
of it many times, and now I know the why.
I am joyously free with no impediments,
to be all that I am capable of in your service.
Time has polished me in ways untold for me to
be rid of all that gets in my way, in your way.

The terrain is like a battlefield, littered with land mines, yet I will let nothing deter me from reaching your side.
I am here, I am now, here I stay forever in your Presence.
In the light and sound and love of the Beloved.

I AM Here.

## One Soul's Passion to Voice its Truth

I have found my voice. What voice?
The voice that sings Soul's song.
The voice that phrases like Billie Holiday,
telling life secrets.
The voice that listens to the heart and tells its story
in words longing to sing forever.

Is the voice true? For me, yes.
Is it objective? Yes.
Is it subjective? Yes.
Is it right? Yes.
Is it wrong? Yes.
Why is this so?

When Soul find Its passion to voice Its truth,
the worlds of duality fade away.
Because, yes BE cause,
when one finds their voice,
Soul sings the sweetest of melodies:
low down blues, sweet jazz, all music of the heart
falls into the eye, the ear, the heart of the beholder.

I soar beyond all things seeking love's expression
through my truth to tell.
Does it enclose itself with love? This I trust is so.
Does it disclose the condition of the heart?
This I also trust.

With this voice I declare to all the heavens who I am,

What I am,
Why I am,
With all the longing within the depth of my being--
lifetimes of living the discipline of love.
Practicing the inner art of silence,
finally after lifetimes I have found my voice.

I can no longer keep silent
as I listen within and play my heart out loud.
I have found the courage to speak my truth
and am blessed with the self-honesty
to stand naked before all, at last; my only garment
the music of God covering me with Sound,
for I have nothing to hide.

By all that is Holy
By all that is good
By God's Grace
Trusting the words articulated through this voice
Can open one's heart to love
to know, to cry, to ache, to see closer within,
inspiring others to recognize something within themselves
that resonates truth,
that restores acceptance of their Divinity.

To be moved one way or another to accept, to reject,
to agree or disagree.
I have found my voice to give gratitude to Spirit
to go within the fire, burning with the steady flame
Of God's love for Soul.

God Loves Me-Soul.
And finding my voice I sing forever the beauty,
the purity, the essence of all Life

Uncluttered, unfettered.

The voice that Spirit releases in Freedom
singing within words, without conditions,
to speak only my truth, through my voice found.

One Soul, one voice, many words, many songs
Of thee I sing.

## I Pour My Heart Out

I pour my heart out to the four winds and the seven seas,
mystical mist clouding memories of why the heart must
empty itself to receive the sweet whispers
of all that is holy.

Yet emptiness is never achieved in one pour
or two, or more, out pouring,
like rain clouds bursting
with life-giving moisture so succulent
and nourishing to seedlings.

Yet...
I pour my heart out, and a waterfall of words
in loving expression
make their way like foot prints on the pages of life.
Whose life? All life.
It is all life living itself in giving
all that it is.

And why this cycle goes on without end...
is because it must do so, for this is its nature,
without ending its beginning is begun.
To know forever what eternity knows
and will never forget what has never been known
until the last drop is poured.

I pour my heart in, listening to the universe
speak its living language to me
in the sound of its pouring.

Yes it is within this sound
that speaks between the lines,
or between the snapping of fingers,
or the silence between the heart beating rhythms.

I continue to pour my heart out into the
vast universal stillness,
into places with no name, for nothing is ever the same,
for now gives birth to each moment ever new.
To experience the same truth in new forms, it discovers
itself within the outpouring of Soul's longing to
blend forever in conscious awareness of the Beloved One.

I pour my heart out in its aching to empty itself
Of all Love, all Life, all thought, for all is in perfect
Accord with God's Will be done, and so,
the giving and receiving,
the outpouring till the last drop begins
filling itself again to heart-bursting moments
of Divine contentment.

Kissing the moment as love is distilled
in the Holy Order of all things beautiful,
blessed with grace, you may ask,
Who is this "I" that claims
I pour my heart out whenever it is filled?
Who is the true pourer of the contents
of contented hearts?
That would be me, Soul.

Yet,
does it matter the who or what it is that has brought Soul
into consciousness awareness of its true nature?
Its purpose here and now, to give and receive

Divine Unconditional Love, for no reason nor rhyme.
For without exception, all things reflect
this Law of Spiritual Reciprocity.

Inhale, exhale, give, receive, outpouring, inpouring,
outcome incoming.
Waves of Spiritual grace nurturing Soul's
expansion of Itself
In God's love.

And so the I AM pouring my heart out,
every last droplet fulfilling Itself,
the awakened selflessness that
through pouring out my heart.
In some small way,
manifests God's Presence in this world.

## Looking Without, Seeing Within

I have found myself contemplating the moon phases
and the night sky, letting the deep stillness embrace me,
gently opening memories, remembrances of other times,
in other places, in other bodies, seeing and hearing
celestial music performed in the dark sacred night.

My heart skips a beat in this moment as I behold within
a sense of loneliness, of longing, of yearning.
I recall all, yes all of the moments, all the places,
in all possible experiences past and present,
when I stood as I am now, in awe, in wonder,
in this reverence.

I recall the wondrous moments of
the creative beauty of the eternal,
and the joyous times in the
presence of the Spiritual Travelers,
standing in the hush of a breathlessness,
as two yellow suns rose in greeting,
heralding the rhythms of new days dawning,
in every Golden Temple,
from the edge of eternity, on the returning wave
of purity of being.
I remember it all.

As this journey of Soul began from the ancient days,
sometimes torn and weary, sometimes a beggar,
other times a thief,
surviving the karmic choices made,

either muddling through, or soaring and inspired,
rejoicing, because I had earned the right to
kiss the hem of the Lord...
I knew then, in that moment, what I know now.

Through the eyes of Soul, I have feasted
on the food of God,
served to me only, as I served the One.

I have been filled with the sustenance of Spirit,
I have distilled spiritual truths, that come
when I remember who and what I am.

Yet I know there is only this moment,
this now, and God-like freedom
must be won in each moment.

And tonight as I contemplated the celestial
movement of moon rising,
stirring within this silent heartbeat, as the moon ever shines,
the rhythmic cycle of fulfilling its mission
in the heavenly space of cosmic dust.

Planets and stars...
moving in keeping with the music of God,
singing sweet lullabies,
awakening all the moments in this Soul journey
beyond space and time, finding as all forms disappear
into vaporized nothings, the Greatness of Soul.

Soul emerges
with the conscious realization,
I was there before the beginning, and I am here,
informed, without form.
Is this the holy transformation of just being love?

All this tonight, swiftly as a butterfly's kiss,
as I beheld the moon and the night sky
in prayerful thanksgiving.
And all the times of forever
that I saw the moon, hearing the prayer
of Divinity echoing throughout all life,
in honor of the great Creator.

What a blessing to Be alive in the worlds of God.

## Original Intent

Is First cause set in motion way back
when the Creator dreamed
and life came into vibrational existence,
creating Soul out of its own substance?

And Soul listened to its calling
Such as God's voice speaking deep inside,
words of Love formed as a question.

*Well, Soul, what is it in your desire to serve Me?*
*What talent is so unequivocally yours,*
*that only you can develop this gift of service*
*to give in service to Me?*
*What is your original intent, aligned with First Cause,*
*Soul, to be in service,*
*discovering your unique talent that only you can give?*

As time goes by in the worlds of man,
lifetimes come and go.
First cause becomes lost into second and third causes,
yet original intent remains in waiting room of labor,
giving birth to itself as intentional, original,
none other like it, only you to fulfill.

Is it easy?
Yes, easier than not fulfilling original intent.
For staying with First cause,
leads the heart to contentment.

I wonder if God said, *Go forth and discover who I am*
*thereby remembering who you are,*
*and know my embrace you never left.*
*Swim with the tides in the ocean of love and mercy*
*Abide in me and I in you, in full consciousness*
*The all in all is all one--*
*LOVE IS ALL.*

# I Trust

If ever, or never, whatever there
is to know or needs knowing,
will always be available,
this requires a trust in Spirit.
This is the secret of an uncluttered mind.

Yes, the secret, the letting go of all the
thoughts restless in their prowling,
growling for attention:
"Pay attention to me, think about me."

All this releases into the wind of
the desire less state bringing
sacred emptiness of silence,
the white translucent moment,
the Now, where only Soul exists.

How is it I—Soul--can know what I don't know?
TRUST~
How have I come to this place of total acceptance?
I know all that comes to me,
each moment, is a gift from the Creator.
How do I know?
How can I not know?

I am not saying the way is easy.
It is fraught with many assaults
which try to stop me in my tracks.

The pain, the illusion of doubt,
the blistering effects of loneliness,
yet knowing all is love.

I see through the shadows of illusion,
and compelled am I to love and serve the Beloved
with every breath, for service is
the air I breathe, the song I sing.

The joy of laughter rises within as
I am chosen to give all that I am and more.
All of this and heaven too.
Yes, this is the gift of trust.
It begins early in life. Consider:
how does a baby know it will awaken
when it falls asleep?

The cycles of rest and ability to awaken to the
call of Soul, inherent in each of us,
through the innate code of trust.
Yes, fulfill the Law of Love
that life teaches as it is lived
each moment, knowing the Spiritual Inheritance
entrusted to each Soul, is birthed within
when we simply learn to trust.
I must trust myself as deeply as God trusts me-Soul.

How beautiful are the wake-up calls
that instill belief in one's own Divinity.
Divine reality sings songs of love throughout
the universe for all to hear and realize.
This is how God speaks to us-Soul,
through celestial melodies, never ending.

Symphonies composed
for the heart to hear and sing forever,

ceaselessly as is the continuous musical
rhythm that vibrates life-affirming sound
cascading like a waterfall out of the River of God,
purifying all hearts receptive
to this music of God,
drowning all illusions,
choking confusion, leaving a clean slate
for Soul to serve life.

Refreshing all life with its clean
notes in the key of living,
trusting, beyond all knowing,
for in listening to the guidance of the Beloved,
whatever is needed within a moment,
within a heartbeat, is here and now.

Soul transcends all limitations
as the giver of service, through the very fabric
of surrender,
claiming no independence,
for it is dependent on God Itself,
for life, love, liberty, the greatest being Love.

Knowing happiness is not a pursuit,
but a state of consciousness bestowed on those
who love and serve the Beloved,
for this is the face of God.

Thank you for the blessing of knowing and trusting--
trust, trust, trust, unwavering, steady as it goes...
one of the many benefits of loving service...to Trust.

## I Wait

Never say never.
Yet before the everlasting gospel of consciousness,
distilled within the heart of joyful
anticipation for what is and
ever was, never lacking, save in
understanding, without a doubt,
what life's all about.

It is never just about you.
The question is, are you being served all you need
in order to fulfill the needs of Spirit?
Ever ready when Spirit calls,
you respond in loving service.
What an honor to be able to hear this biting call.

With a listening heart, poised on eagles' wings,
far seeing with eagle-eyed vision
into all the tapestry weaving,
the fabric of the living breathing
wisdom of the ages, an ancient book,
whose pages are filled with the
experiences of Soul's learning,
Spiritual maturity, and the complete knowing,
in truth of God's love for Soul.

What more could a Servant ask for?
Except, let me be of greater service,
And as always,
I await the inner direction before acting.

## I Wonder

How does one walk through this earth world,
or move through the inner worlds,
without leaving trace evidence of one's passing?

Is it necessary to leave, or not to leave
invisible threads of one's passage?
This I cannot answer; in just speaking for myself,
which is all I can speak for,
In my wake, and in my waking moments,
I strive to not leave behind
any residue that will detain, delay, or detour another
who walks behind me.
Why is this important to me? I don't know,
it just seems so.
And it is ever my intent to not be an impediment
to any Soul in its sacred relationship
with the Beloved One.

Yet, trace elements of love and goodness, humility,
gratitude, laughter, grace, appreciation, contentment--
all the God qualities that may fall in seed form on fertile ground,
in my passing, continue lighting the way of understanding,
not for just my heart,
but for all hearts.
Not just for love, but for all love,
for the lover and the Beloved.
For how can one Soul, except in holographic design,
know the whole that it is?

How? Only by becoming It, by being It!
Deeper within and beyond the wishing element,
past bones and sinews and skin.
Not just under my skin, but deeper, deeper,
never stopping in the quest, in the never-ending study
of Spiritual consciousness.

Upside down, inside out, through the inner worlds,
the sun and moon worlds flicker by as a passing fancy,
yet the hounds of heaven chase me onward.

Do not stop, do not pass go, just be gone in my going.
Consciousness comes through acceptance,
unknown, yet always known,
O seeker of truth, of light and sound, of the reality of
Love's all consuming flame,
into worlds of pure Spirit which devour everything
that does not come from purity of heart.

And a shout is heard, "Please don't follow me,
follow the one whom I am following!"
Through thick and thin, in or out of my skin,
mining for the ancient golden wisdom ever new,
for what is to be remembered,
and some of what is to come,
all recorded in the book of the Experience of Soul.

Though pyramids and wagon wheels
circled within the moon dance and prayer songs,
deliver the language of novels and poetry,
and speech unspoken, of thoughts unbroken,
hear again the stringing of words like a
braided rope not making a lick of sense,
this senseless dialog from the question,

I Wonder, with which this discourse began,
of the footprints of Soul passing through in the journey.

How subtle is the way of the invisible, sight unseen,
the effortless struggle others may call a challenge.

As I walk through muck and mire, the sludge and mud,
this perseverance releases the real wonder of all things
I find, or have found, or to be found,
thus far in this holy place. Why is this?

The Journey begun, never ends,
whether forward or backward, the going is into
the one thing worthy of consideration.

No matter where I AM
or how I got there,
or where I have been.
or how I leave or return...
there is one Truth that abides in the very heart of God:
Divine Unconditional Love.

Yes, the Love, the Love is all, all is Love.
So I say to myself, *Soul remember this.*

No matter how far the travels, or where you go,
or if you stay, each and every moment,
wherever you stand, or sit or lay,
or walk, or crawl, or talk,
you are *always* on holy ground.
No more to seek what has been found,
wherever you go, there you are.

I entered into this world of man,
down from the mountain of God,
and began the search for this very mountain of God!
Yet it takes me far away from whence I came.

For to find the mountain of God, I must turn around,
go back the way I came.
There it is, in all Its majestic splendor,
and the returning climb, awesome.

And if I stumble or fall, or forget,
no matter.
The mountain of God knows my name.
It has always been calling me home.

## Being Right, Or Being in Harmony: Your Choice

Soul takes flight on wings of desperation,
seeking to understand the human condition,
conditional, wrapped tighter than a drum,
yet without the means of communication.

Rather than a rhythm that brings joy within,
unleashed is the lack of rhythm that backlashes
with disruptive energy of one's invalid point of
view, pointless, thoughtless, seeking to undermine
the loving service of others.

Not looking, one cannot see past illusion,
forgetting whatever one sees,
perceives, as foregone conclusions,
has nothing to do with reality. Why?
Have you forgotten life is a mirror,
and everything you see tells you the
condition of your heart?

Let's just ask, Where is the love?
Yes, where is the love, that clears cobwebs
from the eyes, so you can see with the Heart?

If you do this, you may know
the indictment cast by you
came from within the shadows of your heart.
What you see is what you get, no more, no less.
To see love, be love,
to see truth, be truth.

Move softly and gently as an observer,
as one who knows there is always a better way,
and to get there, or here, requires purity
of intent, so I ask, what are your intentions?
I wonder.

## If I Could

If I could love more,
If I could serve more,
If I could give more than I have to give,
If I could generate more ability to manifest
the things of Spirit.
If I could let Holy Spirit use me 24/7 and be conscious of Its
movement through me at all times.
If I found you, Beloved One, waiting for me at the temple gates, open
it I would.
If I could enter your embrace within the softness of two yellow suns
rising,
If I could find beauty within the darkest Soul, whose heart is longing
for the Light,
If I could give without judgment of whom to give to,
If I could know always,
though it is not my decision to know,
just be the love.
If I could, I would not withhold anything
of Myself in love.
If I could, I would not limit Myself in giving God Love, for it is not
mine to keep.
If I could know the unknowable is what is inside of me,
If I could see myself as the Beloved sees me,
If I could change whatever is within me that is not of me,
If I could let Spirit move through me into all the worlds of God
unchanged,
If I could be a reflection of God's True Image,
If I could look into the mirror of God, and see nothing,
If I could know the mirror reflects the light of

ten thousand suns,
If I could know that I am that which I see burning in my eyes,
looking out at me,
If I AM Self-realized, let me be numbered among the God Realized.
If I could know, I am without form, that I too
am the formless,
If I could see the face of God in all things,
If I could give all that I have to anyone who asks,
If I could serve all life with no thought of self,
If I could give unselfishly all that I am,
If I could say, *Do what you will with me*
*each moment of Now,*
If I could do all these things beyond time and space
in this moment of Grace,
I could embrace, without reservation all the love
You give me to give,
I could then say this moment is the moment I am fully awake
in your Presence.
I could then say, thank you, God, for loving my mistakes, and
showing me how to learn from them,
If I could, I would know true honesty is Soul's beginning of the
journey into the heart of God.

## If You Don't Care, Who Will?

God is in the details, yes.
God loves Soul, yes,
Does God care what you eat?
What clothes you wear, what or how you think, or feel?
The myriad choices made on a daily basis, is not
of concern to God, and why?

God loves Soul, Soul is a spark of God.
This is where the attention of God is focused,
On the unfolding of Itself within the Heart of man and
On the awakening of Soul.
God knows that waking up is hard to do.
Staying awake is even harder.

The great trainer, the negative force, stops at nothing
to find ways to drive Soul to distraction, keeping it
entertained through lifetimes of experience, and
one day all its efforts backfire, so to speak,
for Soul becomes strengthened by the distractions.
How in the world could that be you may ask.

There is a compelling element within Soul,
called the Seed of Divine Discontent...
driving Soul onward,
searching, for something, but knowing not what.
Yet recognition is evident whenever a piece of the
Divine puzzle is found, for Soul knows its worth.

Slowly, through these many incarnations, Soul

begins to get the picture, bring it into focus.

Soul begins to care,
Soul begins, not to just see,
but it is gaining Spiritual Insight into its own Divinity.

It begins remembering, and becomes relentless in its
one desire, to find the Beloved One.
Now this is a noble yet laughable pursuit. Why?
How can one find what it already has?

Soul and the Beloved wait patiently for
mental fatigue to set in, and as the
mind's control grows weaker,
the hold it has, to blindside Soul, diminishes.
All the mental escapades indulged in over many
lifetimes, do a turnaround.

They become fodder
for the discovery of Truth, to know the difference
between illusion, and what's real, half truths,
the whole truth and
nothing but the truth.
Now, I surrender my will to you, O Lord.

And God does not care how long this journey has taken,
for the law of opposites no longer pulls
Soul in directions of either or, for or against,
it makes no distinctions.
It has regained residence in its true home
in the high worlds of God.

And Soul, through its persistence,

has earned the keys to the Kingdom,
and they only unlock the door of Service.
All service begins with love, always love.
And here it is...when Soul awakens to Love,
the robe of humility and grace
gently fall upon its shoulders.

Soul cares, and remembers the tender loving care
always bestowed on Soul by God,
from the ocean of love and mercy, is a Love Supreme,
It is God's gift to mankind, it is
The Beloved Master.
Tears of Gratitude fill the Heart of Soul,
for finally, finally,
it knows beyond all knowing,

Soul exists because of God's Love for It.

## Well, Is It?

Life is like memory foam.
Each and every impression, thought,
in each moment impresses itself
like a deposit left behind, left behind
within the fabric of life.

This is one of the many reasons time is illusion,
even if outer structures change within the
outer environment, these impressions left behind
can be read within the sacred text.

What substance of all the converging
energies in this receptacle of this fabric of life...
this started with the question: does memory foam
fall prey to Alzheimer's?

Combining with the elements of reading
the sacred in everyday life,
each moment can be read like pages of a book--
a book of all moments in the passing parade of
the moving river of life--
a library of human and Spiritual experiences
imprinted, waiting for it recognition.

Oh, the stories to be
not just be told, but heard:
a women giving birth, crying out as labor pains assault
her presence of mind,
a flower growing from seedling form sprouting into
the light for warmth and nourishment.

Someone hungry and longing for God fell asleep
in the exhaustion of the journey.
Yes, lay their head down in surrender on this spot of earth
where now a sidewalk covers its instilled memory

and the foot prints of countless Souls
who have walked this way,
leaving behind in their wake: tears, cries, laughter, dreams, hopes,
fears, that carried them through lifetimes, looking for answers
that cannot be found
in just one lifetime.

It takes many, many incarnations
of longing and wanting, and willing to give it all up
and would surrender it all if only the dream would
come into focus...to see clearly...what this empty
longing is about...and why it is all consuming in its relentlessness.

Wishing and beseeching does not bring the answers closer,
yet how can it elude Soul making sincere request?
Ah ha, it cannot!
One of the laws of Spirit is reciprocity,
when sincerity is in the request,
it must respond in kind.

Yet the memory imbedded within the journey of one Soul,
all Souls are there lingering within the very substance of living this
song of all Souls crying out to God...
Can be heard, can you hear it?
Can be felt, can you feel it?
It remains in the sacred book of the heart, all hearts.

It is also the cry in the night
when Soul cries out to God
*Help me, help me, I can't help myself.*

This cry each and every Soul has cried
thousands and thousands of moments out of time,
heard by God, never forgotten by God.

Imagine if you will the grand design in place
to lead each and every Soul willing to surrender
to the will of God,
to a meeting with the Beloved One.

Spiritual discoveries abound within this meeting--
What are they?
All the illusions taken for reality are necessary nothings,
the Divine plan leading Soul to its rightful place
to take up residence within the heart of God's Grace.

But the best is that this is where Soul always existed,
and all the countless struggles necessary
for the refinement,
peeling away Spiritual cataracts from the eye of the beholder,
only because of the moment, that precious moment
of wanting God's Presence more than air,
more than life itself,
For Soul knew It would perish without the Beloved...

The moment Soul knows and declares, *I cannot exist
one more second without God,*
is the moment of greatest discovery:
The Beloved has always been with Soul, all Souls through
incarnation after incarnation,
patiently waiting for Soul to break free of the influence of the mind
and surrender.

How simple it is.
Well, is it?

## It Takes All Kinds, Yet Kindness Gives All

Hello Beloved One, Dear Master,
It's me again...pondering in the late-night hours.
This heart is wondering about many things,
not just cabbages and kings, but matters of the heart.
As children in the ocean of love and mercy,
there are times a Soul finds itself imprisoned by the mind.
With only mercy and grace to lead it out of the maze.

Yes, and it will take Amazing Grace,
when Soul is caught in the blame game,
believing there are rules to the game,
when there is no game, no blame, no fault.

Yes, fault finding will, without a doubt,
only lead to the discovery
of what lies are within oneself.
Truth comes in the wake-up calls,
listen to the caller
and don't shoot the messenger.
Cease talking for heaven's sake.

Listen, Listen, Listen,
Dear Soul, to the heart, not the mind.
Stop blaming yourself or others.
Soul has no-fault insurance,
so take the high road; self honesty prevails when
Soul accepts responsibility for all its actions.
This is the only way history won't repeat itself.

There can be no denial!
How we treat others tells more
about what we hold true within the Temple of the Heart.
Actions speak louder than words.
When Soul loses itself in a sea of anger,
it drowns out its source of Light and Love
in a whirlpool of madness
that outlasts the moments wasted
over nothing, and nothing is worth wasting--
the precious treasures of the heart,
tempered by love, not temper tantrums.

Make a note to remember, temper tantrums have
no place in one who seeks serenity and peace,
for storm clouds of anger and negativity
hide the landscape of the heart.

When purity is speaking, grace is listening.
The whispers of Spirit cannot be heard over
your screams of panic and fear,
yelling the life out of eternity,
so the silent voice of the ONE, who speaks in whispers,
falls unheard,
like tears silently sliding down one's cheek
unnoticed by the Soul who so desperately
needs to hear...
and know just how much they are loved by God.

And so find the strength to surrender the fear,
realizing fear and love cannot
exist in the same place at the same time.

I have discovered, in this world, in this lifetime,
It takes all kinds.

Yet
Kindness gives all.
Love IS ALL.

## Just for Love

*Learn to be more God-like.*
These words have been spoken by the Holy Ones
to their dedicated devotees
who love and serve them, down through the ages.
It is a profound request to willing Souls,
whose one deep desire is to serve the Beloved,
whenever He is within the worlds of God and man.

How important is love?
Love keeps my mind free for God.
A good thing my mind is free in the love...
This love that makes all things new,
old things fade away,
those nothings that seemed so important
can cause one to get lost in yesterdays.

How wonderful that the maze of details
become filled with the clarity of love.
For mind loves those details.
Tales to tell, but when all is said and done,
what is left is love, love that makes all things beautiful,
that brings freedom in its wake,
awakening to the true nature Soul
so bright and beautiful,
allowing Soul to recover the lost moments
clouded by fear,
that tried to imprison Soul in chains of despair,
and the mind did not care.

For the mind loves to pin things down, down, down,
and Soul struggles to open all things into the
Sound and Light of God,
which gives birth to a most beautiful prayer,
a love song to God...HU.

Soul takes flight, for now the mind is free for God.
And the learning continues,
the yearning consumes Soul,
It begins to remember what time has erased.

Soul hears the cry of the eagle and the hawk,
*Break free, break free.*
The chains that bind you are not really there.
The mind wants you to be in agreement
with its mental construct
so it can run the show.
Soul must be in charge of all things
in the worlds of duality.

Thank Goodness the mind has no influence
in the higher worlds,
the worlds where only Soul can journey.
Honor and cherish purity of thought.
Soul must be free from the mind,
So its Heart can be free for Spirit,

I am loved and beloved to the Master
And throughout all this learning, living, loving,
God smiles and universes dance because
A smiling God is a happy God.

Like I know, right?
Does God smile, or cheer us on?

Or rejoice when a Soul breaks through barriers
that have grown rusty from centuries of disuse?
Does God care?

Well, if there is no mercy of which
Soul needs in great abundance, would there be
An Ocean of Love and Mercy?
Would we have the Beloved Master?
And lest we forget,
*Soul exists because of God's love for It.*

So I say, God smiles, but I can't say for sure.
But for sure I have heard the laughter of God.

Yet there is this to consider:
If Soul is happy and content,
If Soul smiles through heartfelt joy,
If Soul learns more about its God-likeness,
If Soul weeps when it knows
the comforting touch of God.
If Soul loves God and manifests Its presence
in the world of Man,
so other Souls recognize this God Love
within themselves,
If Soul, in its journey through the many cycles of
birth and death,
In all the experiences of giving and receiving Divine Love,
would there not be a gift within the heart of this matter?

It is my belief, as we discover, remember, and live
these God Qualities,
as we learn more about living in God's Will
and hearing the Laughter of God,
well, this is just a thought, but perhaps

as we begin to know God in all Its glory and grace,
God begins to know more about Itself in you—
Soul.

Why do I consider this?
God created Soul and placed a piece
or cell of Itself within the heart
of man, and this piece is an unknown
to God until discovered,
uncovered, surrendered to, abided in, and nurtured
through experiences
that keep one growing in love and goodwill.

The Holy Spirit reveals Itself to both the gift,
the giver, and the receiver,
This gift of God that keeps on giving and giving,
And God wants to know Itself within each Soul.

Once the flame is ignited through Soul's awareness
of itself,
Soul becomes more God-like.

We are liberated in this process
So that our very being, our very substance
is now free.
For
Life.

## Do You Have the Time?

What is time?
The measured passage of –
the years go by
moments fly by
quicker than a wink
it is not what one thinks,
And if not-- what is it?

What qualifies timely?
The end of time? Timeless?
No time running out?
The door of consciousness could be a good thing,
if it creates at a moment's notice,
Welcome to Now!

Where Soul exists beyond
the worlds below, where time is measured by
its opposite, sliced up, calculated,
identified by a.m. to p.m.,
four seasons, 12 months, 365 days and nights.
tick-tock the beat of a clock.

Yet underlying all these well thought-out plans of man,
there is the hand of the Divine.
Yes, there is a silent rhythm—cycles within cycles
look to see—see to look–
there it is–
Sacred geometry of all life.
See the sacred in everyday living.

See God's Grace unfolding before one's eyes.
To see miracles requires a receptive heart.
See God language in acts of love and kindness.
Hear the praise of God through poetry, songs,
music, compassion, the gentle wiping
away of a teardrop on someone's cheek.
All this translates the Divine creativity of Soul.
Yes, Spirit moves through the sincerity of an open heart,
tenderly moving into the awakened state.

What a sight to see, the birth of insight transforming
everything into glorious revelation, its message of living:
Have you heard a violet sing?
Have you ever listened to a tree tell its story?
Or a sunrise or setting imagination on fire
with its blessing of eternal ever-changing beauty,
or the power of a storm, the voice of thunder?

When was the last time you looked into the
heart of a morning glory?
Consider:
The spiritual exercises are a race against time,
an improvised solo of one who loves God,
and all the sacred music of living can be heard
in the holy silence.

Step lively, step free, keep on stepping into
the wild blue yonder,
the wildness of God,
to ponder what gifts of Spirit
are hidden to those blinded by
the passions of the mind.

As you know, Dear Soul, a closed heart
closes the portal to the real, the raw;
yet blessed are we who can see,
"it is what it is–"
The Blessings of Holy Spirit.

Note to Soul:
Your Job/Service, should you choose to accept it,
is to enter the world of man
remembering who and what you are,
a free Spirit, breaking loose in love,
endowed with many gifts, an inheritance of lifetimes
of learning love, to invest in all you create,
which is entered into the Book of Life,

You Soul, must survive and do so with the great
sensitivity, endowed with and required by a heart
that never closes.
And with complete vulnerability,
learn to release all the pain endured in your journey,
to pass like shadows in the wind.

Remember this time around nothing will deter you
Because the cycle of changes,
chords of endless melodies playing out loud from the
Heart of God to the edge of eternity,
have taken residence within the heart and sing.

I am a child of the Light and Sound
and I KNOW IT!!!

I am a free Spirit on a sacred journey
weaving the sacredness in the ordinary,

translating the Messages of God,
Communion for me,
into the extraordinary moments in the Life of Soul.

This is indeed a Precious Lifetime.

## Returning Legends

This I heard today: *With every legend is a journey.*
I wonder if it would be more accurate to say,
Every journey is a legend?

Why is it that Spiritual consciousness
comes wrapped in stories?
Stories that touch the heart and waken it to Divine Love?
Stories weave threads of remembering principles
of Holy Spirit within the fiber of our being.

So legends all, Soul Travelers of the far country,
journey beyond the world of man where only
Soul can journey, through timeless legends
before the fall, into divine grace.

No need to wonder how we got here or there
or where in God's name are we,
because the fullness of the Living Word,
in stillness still echoes with the silent prayer song,
that forever pulls the heart strings, forever resonating
our own recognition of the Beloved,
abiding within the Temple of our Heart,
calling each of us to stand united in our strength,
and strengthen our weaknesses, as we love and serve one
another on this sacred journey,
not as legends in our own minds,
but as Souls that have come together as
Spiritual Brothers,
navigating uncharted territory, creating

new legends of Soul Journeys, standing tall, bearing
witness to this miracle of Spiritual magnitude,
Souls, legends beyond time and space...

Brothers who have climbed the mountain of God
and have made the glorious choice to return,
as a way to say thank you to Spirit for
the gift of consciousness.

Why you may ask do they do this?
Because they know one and all,
the difficulty of the climb,
and with selfless service, choose to help other
Souls struggling up this mighty mountain of God
so they may not lose their way...

For those who burn with the holy fire of God's love,
as co-partners with the Beloved
are compelled to light the way for others who love
God greatly.

The beauty of this miracle, is this wave of
loving sacrifice,
and is a legend fulfilling God's will being done...

For to discover the path of the Master,
and the walk to Mastership,
IS the walk back down from the top of
the mountain of God!

Our song has become...silent.

## Morning Thoughts on a Chilly Day

For today and for all time
rests timelessness whose time has come
and gone into heart's fertile ground.

Into the land of listening hearts.
Hearing the sound between the beats.
The interval of stillness in motion,
singing praise of Truth in the sacredness of all things.

Hear
Listen
Listen for the Love
Listen for the rhythm
Listen for the beat
Listen for the freedom
Listen for the song of this planet
Listen for the music of the spheres
Listen for your heart talk
Listen for your eyes to see the great mysteries
Listen for the wisdom speaking truth within the parables of living
Listen for Life
Listen for the beauty
Listen to your breath
Listen for the cries in the night
Listen for the loneliness
Listen for all the goodness
Listen for your feet walking
Listen for all that you are
Listen for the greatness to manifest in the music you are

Listen for the Heart Song of Soul
Listen for the Sacredness that enfolds you in
Its sweet embrace
Listen for the Sound of your tears falling down your cheek to
nourish your heart
Listen for the Dreams that lead you to your true calling
Listen for the Blues and gladly pay your dues
Listen for the sound of giving
Listen for NOW is the time.

# Live Life Unfiltered

Another sign today I saw, and it caught my attention.
*Live Life Unfiltered*--
What would living an unfiltered life mean?
Would it add meaning to life?
what would be filtered out?

Or does this mean
all impurities are filtered out?
Wait, it is unfiltered
so everything would stay as it is, unchanged--
yes, unfiltered, unchanged--
Mind unhinged, doors unhinged, all hinges rust
and scatter like dust in the blowing wind.

Through deserts of a bleak inner life,
lifeless, burned by unfiltered sun
endless ever in its heat, where even
living adaptation requires more of survival mode
out-molded by sheer requirements,
not even preparedness can comprehend.

There is more to survival than surviving
by the hair of the chinny chin chin,
to win each moment in Spirit all day.

What is the only way to stay?
Let love lead the way.
This is the only requirement that provides strength
and longevity in any and all circumstances
devised to test one's courage, one's stamina.

To be here for the long haul, hauling away
debris of lifetimes of cluttered misunderstandings
of what does it take, to embrace vulnerability,
keeping the heart always open to unconditional love.
What can one give in this give and take of life?
Do you notice there is no difference between
everything and nothing?
For life and love
is forever giving unto itself.

Not to keep, unkempt, upkeep, high maintenance
too steep a price too pay.
The hard way bends out of shape
outworn ideas that fall flat
in the desert sand, and swept away by the
wind from the mountain of God,
leaving in its place, from the overview,
is a quietness descending softly into the
hushed moments of life, holding patterns of purity,
hanging out a sign to inform travelers
of stormy weather ahead, and the climb
will challenge every last drop of courage,
encouraging deep consideration before
and after the fact.

Yet fools rush in,
that is what fools are for,
laughing their way into the deep recesses
inside the mountain, safe from wind
and fierce weather patterns, they climb
within the Mountain of God.

And those hanging, dangling by ropes,
on the icy slopes of confusion

which freezes the mind into frozen consciousness,
like frozen popsicles with no flavor,
are left wondering, *where did those fools go?*
commenting on their foolishness,
acknowledging fools rush in where angels
fear to tread.

Fearless fools for God, knowing nothing matters,
having learned early on in their incarnations,
that taking themselves seriously
would lead to excruciating boredom,
boring them to death.

So liberation came early in their incarnations;
laughing at themselves, laughing at life,
filling the Heart with the ability to just go wild loving God.
Giving birth to joyful revelations of a deep secret,
God laughs at them and with them.

And so it goes and goes, unfiltered living,
keeping out nothing that comes to one
to know in its pure state, without confusion,
without illusion, not tampered with or distorted
by the mind.

Soul is open and free to explore the regions of
pristine wilderness of God, and experience unfiltered, or unaltered
by any means, Life.
Fools for God do not want sugar coated anything!

It is unnecessary, and spoils the journey, and so
Souls delight in the unspoiled wilderness,
like a fresh snowfall unmarred by foot prints of any
living being...

Just the fools in all their foolishness, they
honor the path of their travels in the God Worlds.
Leaving no sign of their passing
in regions undisturbed by thought forms or opinions,
they chart their path to the God worlds, unfettered,
unfiltered,
Souls who are fools for God
with nothing to prove, and nothing to lose.
God blesses these fools for God.

## Lost In

Lost in practice, leads to surprising moments
out of times way, no direction known, lends
itself to travel off the beaten path into unknown
territory, the sparkling land of not knowing,
'tis the land of liberation, why? Why?

Well, consider an uncluttered mind, uncluttered heart
beats free and clear with trust in the Beloved,
for Soul knows from past experience
that when and if an unknown needs knowing
it will make itself known in the moment,
so just make yourself comfortable.

It seems to me that Holy Spirit, will take Soul
down to the wire,
before the inner direction comes.
This gives Soul the much needed experience
to embrace Trust and Absolute Reliance
On the Beloved,
until no doubt exists.
Also, this gives Soul the
wonderment and discovery of the Law of Creativity,
which opens the door to the Temple of the Heart.

In this way Soul learns that true freedom comes
when Divine Love and Grace transform
this fragile thing we call life.

## Mastery Moment

There is just the discipline of love.
It must be earned or learn the difference.
For with Divine Love, there is no difference
be and 'tween the lines, for they disappear,
and life is the perfect teacher to try
one's patience,
one's steadfastness
one's purity of heart...
The trials of life can be tried in the court of appeals.

Not so appealing when Mastership is the goal.
No excuses, just clarity of all that rides
the winds of God's breath
transforming all into holy ground.
All life is in this moment in perfect accord,
for in this moment
all is Love,
Love is all.

When Soul awakens to those
precious mastery moments
distilled in the loving heart,
refined in the presence of others,
and the sustaining moment
of Now, is to recognize all,
and nothing at all
fades away into a distant memory.

Days come and go,
thoughts flow out into nothing.
Forgetfulness and remembrance
stay forever tuned to acute awareness
of the fine line that lies between them.

Memory recreates reality, and the
truth remains hidden, clouded by feeling

one's way to the vision clinic, to remove
Spiritual cataracts from insight clearly to
see what Spirit sees, as it flows through me unfettered,
calling me in to account for lack of
discrimination.

No one is above the laws of Spirit...no one.
And yet there is the saving grace.

Yes, Spirit never wastes any opportunity to
bring maturity to Soul.
Yes, all things come
with the training of Soul, leaving no stone unturned,
for through the Law of Economy and the Law of Love,
Soul stands convicted to a life sentence
of service to all life, with love,
and with love all things are possible,

Even Mastering the Moment.

## Grace Notes

It's brand spanking new, never before existed ever
In all eternity, what is this I speak of?
This moment, this NOW,
the continuous renewal of wisdom
harvested through the experiences of Soul.

But experiences are a dime a dozen say the Holy Ones,
so what are the requirements for wisdom
born into its sacred birthright?

Could it be that every act, every effort,
every awakening to sustain itself
within the realm of Grace
needs Soul's conscious awareness,
totally in the moment, conscious of it all?

That is the miracle, the miracle of Now.
Be Here Now, not someplace else.
Where else is there to go, to be?
Wake up and smell the coffee.

Realization, recognition, acceptance
can only become conscious of itself
when one drowns oneself
in the wisdom pool of the ages.

Ageless recognition of all the gifts given in
God's conscious effort,
into the surety, the knowingness of

"I believe this Soul's got It."
Well let's see how life and living manifest
these gifts of the moment.

Being seeing and knowing the one element
that neon lighting heaven's declaration bespeaks
this truth, it is application, how Soul
applies the wisdom given, it must be distilled
deep within the very fiber of being, to claim the gift.
The application of living it, is all it takes to give of
Itself in service.

As one great Soul, Charlie Parker, has said,
"If you don't live it, it won't come out your horn."
God wants Soul to be all that it can Be.
Yes, all the God qualities of Mastership
given, as Soul walks the walk.

To bring the power of Soul into every act,
thought, and deed, each and every moment,
so the world will know who and what you–
Soul truly are; a converter of the God Stuff.

No doubts linger, shadows all gone, Soul has moved
out of the land of unknowing, into the sparkling land
of Holy Spirit, and is free from the
wheel of karmic destiny. Wow!

Dance to the music; breathe every note as it passes
beyond the shores of eternity, making way for new
grace note sound, resonating the music of God
through you as you tune in and tune up your instrument
in alignment with Now...

This brand spanking new moment
that holds the seed of renewal,
the secret of reinvention,
revitalizing life within Soul,
of the living of life's
expression of
Divine love through you, within you,
fulfilling God's will.

These seeds sprout
the wonder of God's love for Soul.

The transcendence of Divine love silently
composes the song of eternity.
Now Is The time.

Transpose Songs of Soul in to the Key of Life

"If you don't live it, it won't come out your horn."

Ever.

## Afternoon Thoughts on a Rainy Day

On this day, like and unlike any other,
I am holding you in my heart thought, Beloved.
For every thought worthy of its name begins with Love.
I behold the eternal nature of our meeting so long ago,
with threads woven into a strengthening bond
to hold forever, withholding nothing.

The future present announcing God's Love,
in which I dwell in the dance of cherished rhythms.
Calling distinctive notes, collective melodies
singing my heart song.

So long this longing, I so longed for Truth
in full measure, filled with God's Beauty and Love,
sending forth on life-giving waves the
ability to swim in the sea of remembering.

Yes, I remember you, You remember me.
O what fun this lifetime is!
Serving in perfect harmony.
Staying balanced in Spirit all day, is like play to me.

I long in this life to stay, to serve.
So I will keep this body fine-tuned
to optimum mode, with high octane fueling
for this vehicle to go the distance
into the Heart of God,
helping all Souls find their way
to the climb of all lifetimes.

I know the way up and down, inside outside.
I must stay in health and wellness,
and good old common sense,
so the greatness of Soul sustains the
agreements of my Golden Contract,

requires me to stay strong.

Surrendered am I, and my choice of longevity
is not because I'm attached to breathing,
just passionate to serve you and all Life
If it be thy Will.

Why do I want this, Beloved?
Because, Now this path is really getting good.
I feel like I am finally getting the hang of it...
make use of me.

The fun is just getting started!

No more struggle, no more strife,
just Divine love to give, to live.
I long to serve you, Beloved. Count me in.
It is said, the tough get going, when the going gets good.

I am so ready, I was born ready
to just go wild loving God.

## The Moving Hand of God

It calls me from beyond my inner worlds
Into the God Worlds

*Calling     Calling     Calling*

Souls longing for God,
their piercing cry in the night,
unanswered,
unless we awaken the warrior within,
whose Sword is love
and Shield is the light and sound of God,
moving in the sureness of the greatness of Soul.

Yes, the movement of graceful recognition
that we are children of the Light and Sound.
As we awaken to all that we are as Soul,
manifesting God's love
like pin points of light in this cold dark universe.

More awakened Souls, more pin points of light.
And as the awakened ones, we keep darkness
at bay, so all Souls have equal opportunity
to answer the call in the night.

When there are more awakened Souls,
critical mass is reached.
Truth explodes into millions of sparkling
nuggets, translucent, golden in its brilliance.

This explosion brings transformation,
opening Hearts to the love God has for Soul,
all Souls.
This brings joy and laughter
in great measure,
and one by one the awakened ones
answer the call, willing to serve all life.

*Calling*     *Calling*     *Calling*

Now being answered.
And Soul finds the sacredness of choice
before them,
Love – Power
Light – Darkness

Let the challenge begin!
We are ready.
We are the moving hand of God
in all the worlds of God's Kingdom.

## No Surprises

Ending forgot the BEginning,
the endless be less what-ness in the
beginning to see the light before
darkness sets.

In the beginning
all things co-existed within the
experimental element of the surprise of the ages,
ageless positions placement without judgment,
in the way critical conclusions are lost in the shuffle,
and nobody is home, no lights are on, cutting corners,
ideas cornered like a rat on a sinking ship, moving in
shipping lanes, collision course of course,
no sunshine when I'm gone, and I am gone so long.

Everyday, in shadows tattooing images
from the dark side of the moon, standing room only,
understanding the risk of overwhelming possibilities,
which are outstanding, waiting for surprise to jump out
of the bag grabbing for the attention deficit well ordered.

For life is full of surprises,
and just when we think we know,
whatever, we find ourselves so surprised to discover
we know nothing.
The hit or miss journey of trial and error
leads one down many byways that force us
to see the good and the beautiful,
just for survival's sake.
Otherwise one could go mad.

There have been times when the senselessness of Life
drives one into the safety of madness, taking a time out.
The path of least resistance surprises one into reality,
which is making sense of the experiences one
finds oneself in, lost in the wandering,
a boat without an oar, up the creek without a paddle,
to paddle our way to freedom.
What a mess 'my will' gets me into.

Soul is left to its own devices, surprising itself
as the Heart awakens to an old song sang true,
heard anew...beckons
Soul into the Light and Sound of Love,
and it knows God can and will surprise the heck out of it
leaving only the pristine beauty of
the Majesty of Soul...

Now comes the test of acceptance, of believing in the
greatness of Soul.
For the residue of the learning element
of surprise, leaves an imprint of unworthiness,
lurking in the shadows trying to convince you
that the shadow world in which the heart
was held captive,
is the real you,
until Soul rises triumphant as it holds
the shield of Truth.

God Loves Me...God Loves Me!!!
It comes first as a surprise, and suddenly the
transformation begins and a Champion of Divine Love
is born out of all the experiences endured in
Its Sacred Journey.

Filled with experiences of hardships and ghost dances,
all the sorrow, the joy, the utter exhaustion,
compel Soul onward,
constantly leading Soul to this moment,
this moment of knowing,
there is no past, no future, only this moment, this now...
and all that was, or is, or will be is here, now.

Wings of Spiritual Divinity dress Soul
with garments of love and strength,
for the journey into the Heart of God begins
this moment, and Soul finds it is no surprise,
to realize when God wants Soul, *ITS Will be done!*
by any and all means necessary,
for all is Love, Love is All

## No Thank You, I'd Rather Be Me

Nonetheless, more or less,
best guess, not to second guess,
one's reason to go through the seasons
of life when it seems treason has the upper
hand, but knowing whatever seems to be,
is most likely another illusion
pretending to be what it is not.

Making statements, true though false,
hiding behind a mask which belies the
unawakened state of consciousness.

What is it that keeps me going and going and going?
It is only God's love for me-Soul, that gives me
reason to get out of bed each morning
and face another day.

I know the moments are not difficult, though
at times my heart aches from the actions of others,
whose only crime is their inability
to love and trust themselves.

For I have learned from experiences of living,
with all the anguish and despair,
there is a deep abiding joyfulness residing within
the chambers of my heart; a fortress of love
nothing can assault or enter,
unless they approach with Divine love.

How blessed am I that, through all the hardships

and challenges life has brought me,
never did even the shadow of
a victim state of consciousness, cast its chains around me
blinding me useless to myself and others.

What a relief to never have had a pity party,
"Boo-hoo, feel sorry for me, for I am not responsible
for my life."
Thank goodness I know nothing has been done to me!
Yet everything that comes to me is tailor-made just for me.

I am not caught in the dreaded trap that can poison Soul.
No way, no how.
Thank you, God for this gift of perception
I bought with hard-earned experiences for
this lifetime journey.

I always knew this time around, it would be for me,
that the hard way would be the easy way.
No holds barred.
There are no victims and life will take no prisoners.

I am a lucky Soul, I was given a head start,
for I believed nothing, nothing until I could prove it
for myself...Yes, I Am That.

And this sense of self, of knowing who I am,
though at times seemed to be in conflict with the
world around me,
in following the beat of my own drummer
whose drumming drummed sense
beyond sound rhythms' sacred vibration,
starting the downbeat of life's song in my heart.

I know the changes, and hey, I even know the words:
Of thee I sing, forever and a day, I welcome the blues
and pay my dues, before they come due
for the planetary rent of the space I occupy and rely on,
to ride out the spin, as gravity passes laws to keep pace
with the pieces, allowing not so much peace of heart,
as the timeless opportunities gifted for Soul,
to master self-surrender and self-reliance in one fell swoop,
learning the Spiritual Law of Divine Love,
and the Law of Economy.

So I sing out loud,
No thanks, I'd rather BE Me!

And where was this discourse of blah blah blah,
going before it got to here?
Coming to this moment, more or less, to find
the best things in life are free.
In my Soul I am free, just waiting to see
what the rest of me costs.

Save the best for last, may just outlast more or less,
less and less, and is there much ado about nothing
from nothing leaves nothing,
save the everlasting gospel, which is something.

Need it be said again, Love is the way, the only way,
to know the greatness of God Love,
the only way into the kingdom of God.
This does bear repeating– Love is All.

All or nothing at all,
God's will Be done.
Each Soul decides the path,

each Soul maps out the journey fast or slow,
lonely, or alone within the great
Divine Loneliness.

And the only seasoning known as the spice of life,
Soul uses liberally, without reason
for any season,
without rhyme or reason,
to satisfy Soul's innate hunger for God.

And as this journey I travel true,
I say, No thanks! I'd rather be me!

## The Observer

Within each Soul is something,
something that is always watching,
making note of all going on in the world
around It, The Observer...
It knows all, sees all.

Its purpose is to be ever ready for
the experiences of life, and welcome them
like old friends, each bringing the
wisdom cultivated by all that is Holy.

Expanding, growing in Its awareness of
the rightness of all things: the harmonies,
rhythms, the innate goodness of Life
as it continuously fulfills its purpose
to observe all things, knowing nothing is personal.

The Observer, the Teacher, is this unit of awareness
that plows the fields of consciousness
in the never-ending study of Spiritual Insight,
becoming enlightened only as it uses it gifts
in application of service to all life.

Otherwise there is no value whatsoever,
unless the keeper of the ancient wisdom
is listened to, and with the listening,
hear heart speak.

Listen as the eyes drink in
the wine of intoxicating purity,
drunk with divine knowing of whatever life is
in the moment, *it don't mean
a thing if it ain't got that swing.*

Although at times consciousness needs a push
as Soul learns the importance of momentum,
for the creative expression of God Love
to manifest Its presence in the dark places of this world,
erasing shadows from the hearts of wounded warriors,
through those chosen vehicles, highly trained
by all that is holy, to be used for reincarnation,
fulfilling the Divine Order, knowing there
must be integrated harmony, in tune with the
starting note of compassion, composing a symphony
of grace notes, and how does this come to be?

Well, I am the Observer, the Watcher, the Recorder,
Keeper of the records of experiences that lead Soul
closer to the Heart of God,
I am the activating of Spirit.

What I discover of truth to behold,
is the reason the blinded eye can see.
Yet with all this, for Soul to awaken to
my indwelling presence, requires a hunger and
loneliness so deep, so all consuming,
nothing else exists, except blessed assurance,
that Without God and Its Beloved,
I, Soul, would perish...

One without the other cannot survive.

God, The Beloved, Spirit, the Observer, Soul,
in musical arrangement, the symphonies composed of all
moments on the edge of eternity,
when the worlds were young, and exhaustion was
a word that had no meaning.
The music of the spheres, whose measured rhythms
are the Heartbeat of Soul...

Its silent refrain sings,
*Come, come, come,*
*closer, yes closer still.*
*The Heart of God*
*awaits you Now,*
*and the Beloved*
*is holding your Heart oh, so tenderly,*
*come*
*closer*
*come*
*Now you know*
*you have not lived a thousand lifetimes in vain.*

## Oh, the Questions

Does the observer just observe?
Or do they make notes—
whole, half, quartered, eighths?

Scattering sound in sacred coverings
scatting the shadows, not just erasing them.
In silence, observe the ingoing and outgoing breath.
Questions pop out of the woodwork...

What is star shine?
Cosmic dust?
*Can someone put me back together again?*
cries Humpty Dumpty,
knowing
all the king's horses and all the king's men
cannot fix what is not broken.

Not even broken promises
washed away by lonely teardrops
drowning out the silence,
trying to make sense out of the senseless.
As golden sentinels stand watch
waiting...

Within the Heart of observation towering
above and beyond until tomorrow,
which, as we know may never come,
as the vagaries of restless endeavors
find solace in the twelfth of never,
which is a long, long, time.

The point being,
where does light go when it fades from view?
And is what is viewed,
faded memories of days gone by?

Defined by the moment of recognition
and acceptance,
seeing is believing.

Is believing seeing?
Sight unseen
insight
out of sight
so take these wings and fly.

Any questions?

## Patience Waiting

Another reason, another season, far flung
over the rainbow where it now hides.
When night time comes, its colors hidden
will be reflected in the morning light
as the dawn of the Spiritual day begins.

Sometimes Soul turns from Its radiance, and hides
outside the realm of the visionary,
that calls forth the mystic within the misty tapestry
of the pageantry of living images
that moves into the stillness,
calling each Soul to discover the true meaning of
service to all life.

And oh, what a joy to learn to wait,
as patience stretches the heart
making room for more understanding,
increasing a greater capacity to give love.

What does it take to walk the walk to Mastership?
It is said it is not a matter of time, but of experiences,
and I say, like a true fool for God, lay it on me,
and I wait for however long or short it takes.

No matter how the gifts of Spirit are wrapped,
I cherish them all.
They are custom-designed just for me, Soul,
uniquely fitted to bring out the best in me,
long as I do not resist but fall head over heels in love
and abide in Love's Way.

Within the process of learning,
the depth of "Do what you will with me,"
means, in truth, in love, in surrender,
letting go of all, save love.
Yes, it always comes up or down to love,
the love that tears out the insides, to cleanse away any
crud that could dim the light of Soul,
for it is coming to know how to abide in God's Love.
It is all good, in perfect accord with God's will.

It is so easy, only the mind wants to make it so difficult.
After centuries, the mind has mastered its game,
making Soul believe all the illusions it spins,
all so real you could swear it is so,
until the dark night of Soul camps out in the
Temple of your heart, and you wonder,
*How long has this been going on?*

Faked out by the mind, mindless dribble, blind-sided,
but a little known tool of Soul is its ability to turn on a dime.
If you choose, you can unchoose;
you have the power of love to renovate the heart,
for though Soul has God-given talent to create,
it can also un-create, begin anew, yes?

The Law of do-overs wins again.
God cannot lose and Soul cannot lose
in the long run,
the reason being whether long or short haul,
when Soul takes mastery over the mind and discovers that
nothing matters, except Its commitment
to give and receive divine love
each and every moment
as we make this life time count.

Keep on keeping on in perfect accord
With God's plan for you—Soul.
In closing, I repeat myself,
Thank you God, I LOVE this Lifetime of Service!

In patience I wait.

## Portal to Compassion

The heart must understand with compassion,
with tenderness, and love.

Yet one might wonder, how is this cultivated,
can it be taught, or caught?
If it can come only when one's heart is open,
never to close again, with conscious awareness
that it is a vessel of learning and fulfillment of
all the experiences life brings, cherishing each as a gift,
showing God's love for Soul, no matter how
the package is wrapped, or what the gift is inside...

Each moment is God-crafted so we become
more God like.
Oh, how strong is a heart in its longing for God?

Each beat is a reminder of how precious is
the gift of life.
Each moment quivers with memories
of the kiss of God's love
imprinted for all eternity.

The mark of God
branded in the hallowed halls where silence speaks
sacred sounds awakening Soul from the slumber
of dreaming itself awake, to answer the call
to Now stand before God,
not to receive anything,
but to give back to life,

to love life compassionately,
completely immersed in serving and giving all
as a magnet of divine love, unconditional in its
presence.

What else is there in life?

## Rest Points in Eternity

What is the meaning of a Heart at rest?
I want to know--
Where is this rest point pointing out the
rest of the story

Ever told at the campfires that
burn across the heavens,
as the storytellers fall silent
deep within a listening prayer.

Down through the ages, each
and every heart restores the stories
of the survival of Soul
as it learns service through life lessons,
in appreciation for all of the belly laughs
from all the yesterdays and tomorrows,
found in dreams, dreamless sleep,
embraced with a certainty,
side splitting, knee slapping, gut wrenching,
burst of laughter and tears, for no reason,
save for the Joy of it.

If you ask where Joy lives,
It lives everywhere, and nowhere;
let all hearts sing
Joy to the World.

## A Rose, A Noble Thorn

The morning is come.
The rose is still blooming.
Silent beauty
reflecting the loving heart of a gardener
in tune with God's grace.
How beautiful is life!

A rose, each petal a story,
the thorn, it, too, a mission to tell.
Writing themselves, stories untold,
yet how telling, how revealing
are they in painting the image and likeness
so true to who they are in creation.
Yet, the condition of the heart sings of life.

What a blessing--
time waits for no one.
Just go on in your illusion of time,
tracking the expensive choices made.
Send out the bill,
let me pay my dues.
I have nothing to lose, nothing to prove.

The moment is where Soul exists
in timeless realms between heart beats,
life unfolding the experiences needed
as decreed by the great teacher,
The Beloved One.

Shown by these gifts, no matter if
they try Soul to the depths of its being,
they are how God says, "I Love You."

What does this mean, an enlightening moment,
that brings Soul beyond the ordinary
into an extraordinary awareness of the
sacred teachings of life as It is lived today?

And if it is gathered up swiftly, in a thimble full,
spilled out, splish-splashing,
every drop falls on fertile ground
and evaporates in the sun.

Yet survival is assured
because the essence of all things interconnects--
stardust and sawdust,
composing symphonies arranged by God
into musical improvisation.

These sounds bring joy to life in this world forever.
Just hearing this music sets hearts to dance
and Soul to laugh
in acceptance of madness,
igniting all the worlds to live in harmony
outside the melodies played many ways
and each note a song of love.

Yet a new dawn paints the day
with colors beyond vibrant,
colors that sing off the charts,
not to begin creation but to continue
what was begun so long ago.
It is recognized in the essence of
The rose.

## Seeing is Believing, Believing is Seeing

But what do I believe?
Yes, what do I belief?
How will I be able to lay my beliefs on the line
if I don't know what they are?

What are my beliefs?
If I am a law unto myself,
what is the law I have laid down
for Soul to live by?

Soul reigns supreme in all things when Love rules.
And where Love is, nothing will ever get the best of Soul.
Love has it all, for all is love.

Can I stand and deliver this truth?
This is my agreement, as Soul.
If not, I won't be able to stand myself.
The law is Love, Love, Love.

As all the books of sacred writings and Divine
mysteries, left behind for Soul to find anew,
are words to live by, and take to heart,
Do as you will, as long as it is within the great law--
Love all things.

This law reigns supreme, the law above all other laws.
No wiggle room, nowhere to hide, nowhere to run.
As the Holy Ones have said since the dawn of time,
Do all with love or don't do it.

Only you and the Beloved know
The condition of your heart.

## Somewhere in Time

Somewhere in time,
share yourself with someone,
somewhere in time.

Somewhere beyond time, beyond
the borders of restlessness, are the timeless
day-mares displacing nightmare visions,
dancing on the shore of eternity.

Somewhere out of time, far out,
near in grace, share with some one
the blessings compassion has taught you,
before forgetfulness sets in.

In other words, leaving empty spaces between
letters that weave understanding
outstanding words that paint worlds of possibilities,
arrested sentences from whence they never came,
are here just the same.

Somewhere, nowhere, anywhere, everywhere,
seekers search for meaning of what makes sense.
For all one knows is, well, not much if
one stops to think about it.
Don't you know, better not to think
those thoughtless thoughts tumbling down,
down the rabbit hole.

Lightening strikes twice

burning away patterns that deny Spiritual destiny.
Yet denial is not an option.
Get it, got it, forget it, going for it and yet, forsaking,
the true, real, who you are.

Give yourself a break, cut yourself some slack.
Spirituality requires a knack that knocks loose
crusted, cemented, stonewalled, and stalled,
jury dead-locked,
deciding evidence beyond reasonable doubts.

Doubting Thomas declaring, show me the bill,
what price to pay for Spiritual ignorance,
drowning in arrogance, retarded misconceptions,
no excuse, the law is the law, letter vs. Spirit.

Somewhere, somewhere, out there, in here, the
sharing is easy, serving is easy, in the compassionate
wayfaring adventures of the Spiritual travelers.
All for one, that band of Brotherhood,
yes, the far seeing ones, delighting in each moment.

Stay hungry for Soul food—
nourishment of heart and Spirit.
Feed Soul naked truth supplements
on sale as we sail through the cosmic seas
to become one for all again, and again,
sacred sharing.
What are the elusive moments of knowing
beyond reasonable doubt?

There is certainty
of countless ways of counting blessings
brought to Soul each moment.

Only games have leader boards.
Life is not a game; could be a test.
Somewhere in time it is found, life is real.

So reach out and touch someone, love multiplies itself.
You find that someone shared of themselves,
when it was most needed, a lifesaver,
just in time for you to remember, that what was shared,
was something you shared with someone,
somewhere in time, stirring Soul memory, Wow!
That someone is you, guilty or innocent
as charged, to serve with Divine Love.

Rising in the morning mist of a new Spiritual day,
new beginnings, start-up menu, the icons of
one's life, lifting higher, and higher, always
standing on holy ground.

The jury is in.
The sentence is nothing less than
a lifetime sentence; it is so Divinely Ordered...
No time off for bad behavior, or good behavior,
it is all the same,
serving all life through compassion
somewhere in time.

## *Soul Survivor*

Standing tall, seeing far, far seeing, seeing more,
It fades away in the morning light,
dweller on the threshold, seeing out
over the face of the void, the endless void
that separates the worlds of man.

Struggling in his human consciousness,
anchored by fear of the unknown.
Yet the relentless urging for Spiritual liberation
gives Soul the strength to cross the void,
into Soul's true home.

God in his Kingdom comes and
welcomes each weary traveler,
greeting Soul in the Name of all that is Holy,
celebrating its journey in consciousness
into one of the worlds of Heaven.

Seeking to know all of itself, the who, and what it truly is,
in answer to the age-old question "Who am I?"
Soul, a sparkling unit of awareness,
crosses the threshold into the light of a thousand suns.
And for once, knows, beyond a doubt,
this light is Its Light!

Wonder of wonders, how can this beauty of me exist?
Yet with a doubt, it does
Yes, I AM Soul!
and beyond time and space, this is my home.

Yet my desire to know more, be more, has sent me
into the world of man,
to learn, to serve, to love,
no matter what illusions come to deter me,
or interfere in my journey into the heart of God.

Learning the gentle art of patience
will smooth the way and make the journey easier.
Already I have learned the importance of a giving heart.

And closer I move on, beyond the shores of eternity,
into my true home,
not as a visitor, but as a full-fledged citizen
of the worlds where all Souls live and move
and have their being
in the sweet nectar of God's Love for Soul.

## Soul Knows what the Mind Cannot Comprehend

The biting cold, the merciless wind erases the cries
of Divine Discontent rising from within the center
of Heartfelt discomfort.
No hope of rescue,
no chance of relief from the elemental
changes that assail and assault my very existence,
will I die in this frozen waste land?

It won't be the first time,
and most likely not the last.
If only experiences did not escape my remembering:
Carry on, they command,
stay the course, they demand,
in this God forsaken land.

Soul forgets to remember.
Yet it must remember all its lifetime travels,
making all its incarnations count.
Knowing creativity must speak as a living
language of love.
It is not always the struggle that strangles
creature comforts.
Sometimes the wheel of life settles on other challenges--
the ones that rip the very heart from resting places.

Soul must rise to all occasions,
for every experience brings opportunities
for Soul to know more of itself
and Its relationship with God.

The time is past for picking and choosing
what you want...for Spirit always gives what Soul needs
nothing more nothing less.
Accept all the gifts, do not keep God waiting.

The gamut of the human condition is set up for
the greatest of learning; the lessons bittersweet,
and no amount of begging or pleading will
remove it from your Grace.
All things are of Spirit.

And if Soul truly loves
each of the gifts of Spirit,
nothing will keep it from its true home.
For even when taking leave,
Soul has never left its God given right.
Soul always lives in the high worlds of God,
and forgetting is not an option.

Train Soul in the ways of Spirit:
Become the rememberer,
Become one of the far-seeing ones.
Stand on the shoulders of Giants.

Climb the mountain of God and sing
with a Voice from the Heart of Love,
praising God with its Heart song, HU.
It will reverberate throughout the heavens
calling all Souls to lift up their voices
and sing the celestial melody forever.
So I cross my heart and hope to die
if this Love song of God is not Truth.

## Sound Freedom

Why is it some spend their days seeking
To fill their life with meaning,
And others seek the emptying of meaningless,
unnecessary distractions that get in the way of
true meaning, the emptiness, the deep sacred silence,
the portal that leads to the Heart of Love.

The silence births its sound into the
Soul of drum beats, heart beats, Soul speaks.
Jazz freely given spontaneously improvised,
The very secret of it all, in the moment,
leading the listener to go beyond sound
into the stillness, into the silence that gives form.

Hearing not just the notes,
knowing Soul plays its instrument of choice
in expressing its deepest knowingness,
proclaiming the joys and sorrows and struggles
and triumphs of Spirit, telling it like it is,
coming to know itself.

Soul speaks, the angels sing,
happy feet jump in joyful recognition,
grateful in knowing we are not alone,
striving to embrace the emptiness for it to be
filled with the golden nectar singing each drop.

Why sing, why love, why play your instrument?
One of the Holy Books says, "make a joyful
noise unto the lord."

God, in keeping Its promise to Soul:
You are my heartbeat, you are my sound,
hear me, hear me, listen to my sound
lighting the way, into the deepest part of you,
never before known, until you solo,
improvise your life, in accordance to Love's true
creativity, never before created until this moment.

Let it rip, let it sing, note for note,
"A Love Supreme."
Coltrane knew the questions to ask,
he played the answers with melting love
and as the listening heart
he knew truth.

Truth woven into the very heart of sound,
and beyond sound is the source of the sacred
HU, embedded in all sound that springs from this
well of silence, so deep, so quietly moving into
waiting hearts longing for the unnamed, the no thing.

The all in all things, within this Heart of HU--
Hear it
Know it
Be it
Love IT!

## Is There a Spiritual Law of Do-Overs?

To begin anew, undo, renew, do over,
under buttermilk skies...
keeping the eye of God on me please.

Go in, go without, down and out for the count,
will it ever add up? What?
Life, will it ever make sense?
I doubt it, because I don't think life is supposed to
make sense, that is, and why?

Because life is a random walk among the stars,
it is anyone's guess where the direction goes;
all you can count on is the going part.
Soul must stay strong so the mind does not mislead,
and the choice is to follow where Spirit leads.

Topsy-turvy as this world may seem
on the outside looking in.
God's plan for Soul is impeccable in its
design, greater than the celestial wonders
day-scaping, night-scaping, no escaping what has been
written in your golden contract, sign sealed delivered.

No amendments, and so this wonderful adventure
throughout eternity is blessed and sanctified by
the living truth of the matter.
And what is better, to be found wanting?
Or not to be found, and still wanting.
And why is that?

Well Soul has been given everything;
all the Spiritual gifts, all of them,
from the beginning of its first meeting with the Beloved.
No wonder the wise ones say, *one's state of consciousness
is one's state of acceptance!*

This journey of Spiritual discovery
is teaching me to be more God-like.
Soul soon discovers, no one will go far,
without finding a way to say thank you
to Spirit for this gift of consciousness.

Somehow, as a Spiritual Traveler
moving through this world, I knew
there would be no substance without Service
to God.
For to know God is to Serve God,
and in so doing, in so being, I find myself within
the Heart of God.

These words strung together would sound empty
indeed, were they not imbued with an
unconditional loving heart,
always reaching beyond the known,
delighting in the unknown.
There is always more, always one more step,
one more heart longing to know its own Divinity.

The task is clear—
Keep going where the Beloved has need of you.
You know nothing is about you, ever.
If it were, there would be nothing for you to learn,
and we would not need the Spiritual Law of Do-Overs.

## The Spiritual Law of Exchange

If you don't inhale, you can't exhale.
I speak of the breath of life, in and out,
out into the dawning of consciousness,
of forgotten worlds upon worlds.
What's going on in your galaxy?
Pray tell, do you have more time?
Or is your time running out
to get the message life sings to you?

Love is the only way to go or stay.
Beyond the blue horizon, where stars playing outshine
the noon day sun blinding the eye,
sight unseen, longing to see where beauty is,
beholding what it is, and what it looks like.

Calling, calling, do you know how to
answer this call of Soul?
Please, Listen out loud.
Can you hear the earth song?
The heart song?
The call to awakening song?
The silent song so long ago sung
singing in the night, into the light
with no ears to hear?

The sounding lament fades into the falling night.
Refrain so sad, so sad, you don't even know my name.
Yet forever I shall sing haunting melodies
of laughter and tears.

Forever I wait for ears to hear and
hearts to recognize the notes,
resonating within the beauty of Spirit's embrace.
Exquisite ecstasy, bittersweet remembrance--

It's not too late; it is never too late,
for time and eternity stand still
in waiting, as Soul goes into the heart
of the fierce winds
blowing conscious awareness into the moment,
and so it is,
skin ripped and shredded,
then mended by the golden thread.

And the knowing, the knowing, Beloved one,
of your Presence.
I know I will never stop loving you,
or life, for in your Presence I am who I am
because you love me.

Yet, why is Soul kept apart from Its truth song?
Listening, I hear it, hearing I listen.
Show me, God, what I am missing
before it is too late.
Break the heart into millions of pieces,
fragmented like a puzzle, waiting for your direction
for me to bring the missing pieces together again,
where the sun does not set and the stars cry crystal tears.
falling into universal stillness
impregnating silence with the gift of My Truth
For crying out loud...

Expressions of formless reality of the spoken and
unspoken sound.

Truth begotten through the pregnant pause as it
inhales and exhales,
revealing the silence between the Breath,
the sweet taste of loneliness deep in the recesses
of all that has been forgotten,
now to be remembered.

It is mine; it is the birthright of all Souls.
It is the Creator, loving all its creation.
It is life, it is living, it is birthing,
it is in labor, contracting, to breathe.

Soul intoxicated forever
as the Creator gives life to all that is,
In all the worlds,
endless expressions of Itself, no two alike.

In one moment, push, breathe, a new day is born;
I am still here.
It is time to move on.
I am coming, I am listening.
Yes, I care,
Yes, Yes, Yes.
It is time for the eagle to fly everywhere
the wind of Spirit blows.

Souls Knows:
I am listening, no more forgetting.
For the Heart, is now the living Temple of Soul.

## *Standing on the Shoulders of Giants*

Each and every moment is sacred,
in witnessing the sacred in everyday living
on Holy Ground, On Higher Ground.

We have the honor to stand on the shoulders of Giants,
so we can see farther than others,
becoming the tribe of the "Far Seeing Ones"
The eagle-eyed adepts.

Flying high, soaring with eagle hearts
We can see what God Sees.
Looking out we see all things,
yet to see what God sees, we must turn our vision
into ourselves as well,
To see what is seeing.

## *Purity of Intention*

Today these words caught the attention of my heart
in flight: "Purity of Intention."
How profoundly beautiful is the wisdom
with such depth of simplicity, contained in these words.

Intending to follow this sign post from God,
directing Soul to take lead to follow to where
God is intending It to contemplatively consider,
What is Purity of Intention?

Within the purity of heart, a loving heart begins
beating rhythm, without ending.
How this simple phrase lights the way
showing all thoughts beginning
in purity of intention.
Thought word and deed, yes indeed, must be
Love realized.

Where integrity and generosity of Spirit are nurtured and fertilized
with fragile tenderness,
tenderized, purified in consciousness,
multi-layered, multi-hued with rays of life giving fragrance to
behold the beautiful strength
of Grace and Purity, so cleanly scrubbed and shining,
taking away all the clutter left behind in just one day
of living, before it gets in the way of seeing clearly
how humility enfolds a heart that is pure.

How strong is the strength of Purity?

Only those who are pure of heart
can stand within the Holy Fire and not burn--
just feel the heat,
causing only the melting of a heart born to love.

Only the pure of Heart can see the face of God,
and not have madness become their companion
for lifetimes.
Only the pure of Heart see no evil.

Only with Purity of Intention, immersed within
the sanctuary of one's heart,
can Soul withstand all that comes
to batter and assault Its very being
with unimaginable forces, creating great challenges,
as the mountain of God they climb,
with purity of intention.

## Sun Rising Destiny

The unfolding of a quiet day--
morning sunrise over sand and ocean,
contemplation of the Living Word,
it shows me the learning can come only
through surrender and a loving heart so immersed
in its love for God,
all things pale in comparison.

With illusion's departure,
there is nothing to compare.
I do not dare.

Treading lightly on sacred ground,
following the haunting call of Soul,
traveling in the high worlds of God's grace,
and this place I would stay
until service calls me away and beyond.

Yet I am learning how to be multidimensional;
to stay and go without taking leave,
to be in all places, to be all things of Spirit.

Ready whenever needed, however needed,
each moment in God's time in spite of me.
Flawed though I may be, I still answer the call
of service, for of myself I can do nothing.

And if I felt perfection a requirement to serve the Beloved,
I would die before I wake.

## *All Truth is Found in the Moment vs. Instant Gratification*

It is said by the Holy Ones
that the Temple within is the greatest
temple of all.
It is where Soul finds wisdom,
peace, love, joy, freedom and true happiness.

This temple is a mystery; yet is not secret
to those who find the way within the hidden
stillness resonating within the heart.

I have been offered truth everlasting,
yet misled was I in assuming it would
descend into the consciousness instantaneously,
and I, Soul, would be instantly transformed
in consciousness.

What escaped notice was the is
and is not of Spiritual transformation.
For when Divine Truth kissed me on the cheek,
I waited breathlessly for the transforming to begin
in the moment and end in the moment.

I had to learn, that yes, in that moment of the kiss of truth,
leaving its scar upon the heart,
I was transformed.
Yet the deformities of my meager awareness
and understanding,

were pitiful companions to the awakenings

that began to stir in the temple within.

As time brought a deepening realization,
I see me now, and look at the me then,
filled with unearned expectations,
and I see beyond
the barriers of time's illusion, and can say
the vast transformation begun long ago did happen,
though it required making many trips to the
temple within, to know love, to know God,
to know there is nothing to know save love.

From this vantage point of now, I realize that
each trip I took to the temple within,
little by little expanded this holy sanctuary,
and in the stillness within the sound and light of God,
the expansion of consciousness slowly
grew into the recognition of the Greatness of Soul
and each trip left the fingerprints of God
within the songs of the heart as it
sang chamber music caressing
each note, each trip, each seeking,
each surrendering, all the gifts of Spirit
that passed through this heart kissing it
on its passage out into the world.

Each moment of grace has indeed transformed
the temple within into a majestic cathedral of the heart
just from that one moment long ago when
I stopped
my world
to listen to the Master's Voice.

## Thank You God for Everything Just the Way it Is

Some say to me, out of love and concern,
"Oh my dear, your life is out of control,
it is just too hard. How can you stand it?
How can you survive this constant battering,
without let up?
What kind of world do you live in?"

When looking at outer conditions,
the illusions are running amok.
But look behind the illusions, see God's hand at work,
shaping my world, my life.
And for this I say,
Thank you, God for everything just the way it is.
I love my life!
When I see my life, both inner and outer,
I see movement and grace and experiences that show me
how much God must love me.

What is truth? What is illusion? What is real?
Only Love is real; all else is illusion.
Everything, everything fabricated and manifesting
in these worlds of duality is illusion.
Anything that qualifies itself with an opposite is not truth,
for truth of itself, stands alone, has no opposite.

So I say, just see love, no matter how
experiences of the day are wrapped.
It is said in the Holy works that
Soul must have every experience for Mastership.

I ask for whatever it takes.
So here I am on the razors' edge of consciousness,
sometimes with painful awareness of a hurting heart,
due to misjudgments cast upon me.
Yet I have learned, what others think of me
is surely their problem, not mine.
This I remember most of the time,
sometimes attention lights for just a moment or two,
and my heart feels sad.
Then Soul gently reminds me, Let go, let God.

It is great to sing boohoo blues
just don't be the boohoo whiner.
Remember what it cost you to be who
and where you are this moment.
The dedication you have to give service,
gave you strength and the courage to banish fear.

This is something that is learned the hard way,
and the price is high, especially for those
teetering on the edge of Spiritual bankruptcy.
Yet only love can save them from themselves.
Fear rules the dark night of Soul.

For some, it may not happen overnight,
or in a lifetime, no hurry, no time,
just rhythms of sacred geometry.
It stands to reason, if they could do better
they would, if they could love more they would.

Cast the shackles of the ego and bow before
the great unknown, and the Beloved knows,
life will teach you better.

It is also true, if one says they are love,

compassion, caring, and a tenderhearted servant
of all Life, this will be all they could see in the
world around them.
Be kind to all, especially yourself,
and forego time spent judging others,
or pointing out where a faint-hearted Soul falls.

Forget not, they are seeing themselves in others,
so rather than grabbing the hook of judgment,
ask, *Am I helping or hindering a Soul in its*
*search for the Beloved One?*

And bless us all, for are we not here to
lead the seeker to the feet of the Beloved Master?
What a wonderful lifetime,
what wonderful opportunities.
Contemplate this,
how many lifetimes have we incarnated,
chasing the will o wisp of Spiritual Liberation?

It eludes us for lifetimes; we can almost touch it,
feel it, taste it, yet leave another lifetime
with Divine Discontent breaking our hearts.
We come back again and again, seeking, wondering,
where is this freedom, this Spiritual liberation that
stays out of reach?
And one day, in a lifetime, we pass someone
and they smile,
and the love in their eyes awakens Soul within.
Dare we consider, this lifetime we just might make it?

We are learning how to make all our incarnations count.
This is indeed a precious lifetime.
If you have been blessed to carry a sword and shield,

you have learned the sword has a double edge:
one side wounds, one side heals.

In leaving this wandering poem, I will share
a golden nugget given me in a precious moment
by the Beloved One.

"Remember, if you pull your sword you must use it,
and if you use it, do so with love,
and when you sheath it, do so with honor."

We, the awakened ones, have been charged
to work and serve with Love
from the Heart of HU,
Lets keep the garden of our consciousness in order,
singing songs of Divine Love as
we discover an old truth in a new form.

Beauty truly is in the eye of the beholder.
And if chaos appears to rule my life,
Double-check what you are seeing...
for of a Truth,
I am content.

Thank you, God for everything, just the way it is.

## *The Art of Silence*

To the silence I sing of the listening heart;
to the heart I sing of broken hearts
that grow bigger when breaking,
making room for more love
to fill leftover emptiness.

In praise of practicing the art of silence~
in tune with all sounds deeper, deeper into stillness born,
not yet birthed into reality,
for a banquet I must attend, to earn entry
into the hallowed halls of nowhere else to go.

To find questions forgotten long ago when
answers filled the wonder of it all,
never made sense; for without questions
befitting the quest, answer me this~
Is it the Heart leading the direction,
before the journey begins?

Again and again over the rainbow's ending
somewhere beyond the river of timeless waiting,
it is over and under the spell cast by the hush of eventide
to abide in the House of the Lord
forever, never to part.

Departing, it goes, going, gone back to
songs sung within the deep recesses
of the silent heart filled with longing so
long remembered, the haunting refrain

engorged on the silent mysteries within
that await the fools who are blessed with compassion
and have learned what death knows.

What could death know when,
with its' dying breath sends an invitation
for the transformation to begin on the downbeat,
the continuous journey sustained with purity and love,
hand in hand with the Beloved,
finding the journey never ends; it is as ever changing
as cloud formations moving in and out and away
in harmony with the wind, and rain, discovering
nothing is wasted.

Every drop, every cell, every molecule
dances with in the Law of Economy,
for as time waits for no one, Spirit never wastes
any opportunity to bring maturity to Soul.

Listening to Holy Spirit singing songs of silence,
life continues in tune with the harmony of truth,
discovering no opposites to break the stillness
within the listening heart, living the art of silence.

For here in this sacred chamber of secret longing,
the discovery of Soul's true being is birthed
again and again, born, formed, formless, transformed,
kissed by silence, finds its essence, Itself, and knows,
This Is What I AM, and have always been, this radiant form
created in the likeness of God Love.

The All in All for All Souls wondering, in their
wandering travels in the silent spaces,
and places, without name, or needs.
Nothing, just purity.

Blindness takes flight, scales fall from the All Seeing Eye,
hearing all sound, for it comes from the silent stillness
where songs of the heart are whispered through images
of love's refrain...
waiting for those who can hear...
to listen.

## Awakened Heart

If ever I would find myself to lose the very
essence of life's meaning without meaning,
knowing the difference, if ever the need arises,
to fly beyond the starry night.

Questions come as thoughts.
What is beyond the Sound?
Yes, what lies revealed in sacred truth?
Stories revealing secret teachings,
as we bow before the Beloved Teacher of forever.
Of the ongoing never-ending study of Spiritual disciplines
revealed in the Way of the Eternal.

Soul's experience of life and living,
of all the sorrow and joy required to learn,
leaving no stone unturned.
Yes, Soul must go through every experience
to know Mastership.
Yes, no detours around the block.

Elemental changes occur
when the awakened Heart emerges from fog of distant dreams,
shining light on truths discovered
long ago, without a moment's notice,
on silent feet.

Footsteps echo on the horizon,
Wise ones waiting with life jackets of Wisdom,
wisdom of all that is now and ever was.

Only HU will transform the Heart,
fine tuned in the Art of Listening,
within the Art of Silence,
where sacred sounds are heard.
Only then is Soul awakened.

## The Future of the Past

Today these words caught my eye.
The Future of the Past
Is long gone into yesterday's tomorrows.

Lessons caught or not, for
Life, Love and Living cannot be taught,
only experienced within the heart of all things.

Rejoice in gladness, and sadness, it is all the same
to me, for I will soon be free of the snares
that try to create differences,
if not already, for the future is past all limitations.

Can't see what is hidden in the mind's eye,
Looking to the future in what is past conception.
Insight's reception singing about the rings around
the circles, jelly rolling joy into now...
All is here now, past, present, future,
Depending upon your view pointing the way
of seeing, what it is, what it looks like.

And golden coins unseen fall into the sands of time
waiting for discovery which comes forever new.
I have seen the future; it has come to pass in all its mourning glory.

The continuum of Soul's journey without ending,
begun before time began its illusionary stand.
How outstanding it is to know before
everything was, I was.

Yes I was there, here,
when God birthed Itself in universal stillness.

The sound echoed within my heart,
and though startled I was, I was pure knowingness
that I am the beginning, with no ending, with no past
or future to Now, invest within consciousness,
like rainfall splattering within the atoms,
splitting apart in unison,
shattering wake-up call to all Souls,
come before you leave,
rising like the sun to the call of service.

Why am I here? To give and receive love,
and in this process of Spiritual testing,
discover I-Soul, give and receive of myself in tender accord
with God's will is done and I am done in Love,
I AM Love.

I greet life Now, not then, nor when;
no excuses ever, forever more.
And the future of the past passes away
Like a pregnant pause, knowing all
Is love.

Yes I get it? The future of the past is here now,
within the Heart of Hearts
Beating the rhythm of God awake in me.

## The Line Between Divinity and Madness

The thin line between Divinity and madness--
where did it disappear to?
Or did it?
Maybe I just don't know any more,
which is more likely than not,
especially for one such as me
who lives on the edge and goes back and forth
many times like a yo-yo confusing itself
with a ping pong ball.

No matter, for this time, over the edge I am gone
into nowhere land without a clue, or even a paddle
and no water anyway....and no mystery either.

The stark landscape belies itself in tattered displays,
withering grasses, limbless trees, not even
empty bird nests survive this wasteland.
Over the edge, turning around merry-go-round
to the edge.
Don't go too far; stay on the edge in keeping with
the plea of madness.

I take a trip within to find where I am,
yet have never been where I am,
way out, it is a moment of arrival,
finding now between the fine line
of Divinity and Madness.
and no matter which side of the line Soul is found
in finding God,

Soul is still left with the passion of just going wild,
going mad, loving God.

If anyone who longs for God, had a choice between
Divinity and madness, they know the line disappears
in the light of a new Spiritual day,
for either choice is but a hair's breadth,
for Divinity is madness,
madness is Divinity.

Remember...
the ride is just begun, so hang on and go
where no Soul has ever gone before or after
to find the Heart of God,
and feel the touch of God's Hand
as I travel on without question,
I no longer care that I care
for I am mad in the Heart of Divinity.

## The Lone Stranger

Here I am,
The lone stranger
In a strange land, a barren land.
Am I forgotten? Can't be! I know who I AM
In this hope-forsaken land.
I AM not lost,
I'm not alone.
Even though no direction known,
Like a rolling stone,
gathering no moss as I move while standing still.

In the stillness of the night,
darkness embraces me,
love erases me,
into the formless.

This excruciatingly painful knowing,
that rips to shreds any thought that
I know It All. HA!
I know nothing, I Am nothing,
I can do nothing except by the Grace of God.

And so I die to live to love--
one of God's misfits,
stranger than fiction,
This story of the lone stranger.

Written and recorded in the book of the heart,
I am the lone stranger.

## The Mind is Going Down

The defeat of the mind,
the moment of mental waterloo,
when it occurs with meltdown splendor,
is an epic moment in the unfolding of Soul,
moving Soul up on survival scale.
Why is this?

Because a surrendered mind is a true servant,
subservient to Spiritual purification,
for it begins its true expression
of love for all life,
going forth in total agreement,
with full acceptance for all that is required
in a moment's notice, staying in love's way.

Freed from all impediments that stand in the way
of understanding the gifts of conscious
revelation of what this lifetime is about
and why Soul reincarnated this lifetime,
integrating all its incarnations in one fell swoop,
knowing without the mind's doubting deceptions,
*Soul exists because God loves it.*
This alone is more than enough for liberation
this lifetime.

Straight, no chaser, Soul is ahead of the game,
no stopping in the sticky glue of time's track,
for this time is timeless with Divine clarity,
just go wild loving God.

Celebrate the Divinity of all life,
for to be in the presence of the Beloved
touches Soul in ways profoundly sacred
as the heart is kissed by grace.

Soul, free and clear in pristine wilderness leading
its way forever within the solitude of the alone,
yet never knowing loneliness.
So blessed with knowing all things worthy of love,
embracing all life unfolding in its light,
displaying loveliness, breathtaking,
to behold beauty in the eye of God,
whose vision encompasses all songs singing praises, phrases,
pure sounding music...reminiscent of Lady sings the blues.

Touches deep,
yet deeper still, hear the stillness
at the altar of silence,
a hymn to God's thrilling touch in all things.

All things are touched and imprinted with this
searing love, whose fingerprints give life
meaning to sacred whispers unfiltered within
an awakening to truth.

It is the Beloved in concert,
holding forth within the chamber of the heart
of all living, vibrating eternal rhythms
composed in words of love, yes of love.

Soul sings like the wind-scape of stars and cosmic dust
and birdsong, in unison with crickets cricking
and the red-red robin comes bob-bob-bobbing along.

Long way to go when there is no longer anywhere to go.
Soul lives in the high worlds of God
In the present moment.

Suffice to say, the journey ends before it has begun,
with many beginnings and endings, woven in the delicate fabric,
the stories of Soul's journey triumphant at last,
knowing with purity and simplicity,
Love is All, All is Love.

As the arrow points its informative direction,
"You are Here."
If you lived Here, you would be home now."

Are you laughing yet?

There is no sound so joyful as the laughter of God
and the Sound of HU.

## Moment

In the moment, it all comes down to each moment,
and the choice to greet each moment with love,
with no agenda, just pure undiluted, unconditional love.

This is the only way that brings sense to this
wild, wonderful, weird world
we live, move and have our being in.
Can we go forth and lead an unscripted life
from this moment forward or backward?

How real is the unreality of existence filled
with all the drama, aches and pains
perceived as personal assaults against well being?
How dare he, we, they, us, them do this or that?

The complaining reaches out into the universe and
travels round magnetic poles and becomes static,
which no one listens to unless it is personal.

Nothing is personal, it is nothing;
no name, no face, no place.
Only love's saving grace bringing peace upon
the stillness residing within the heart:
The listening heart,
The loving heart,
The giving heart,
The breaking heart,
The healing heart
The understanding heart.

Wrap your troubles in dreams.
Wrap your dreams in love.
Unwrap your life in love's embrace.
No matter what happens all over the place,
what matters is the internal attitudes,
held deep in the heart.

Whatever changes manifest within this world of man,
no matter what key or chord or sound is sung or played,
no matter what instrument the music is played through
in its expression, each note
must be distilled through the heart of love.

All thoughts, words, deeds, misdeeds, mistakes,
make no mistake, all survival hangs by a thread
which derives its strength through love and love alone.

How important is love?
Try breathing without love.
Try singing without love,
or being without love.

This force, this love, this power,
Is God, and God is Love.
And its mercy is the Beloved One,
whose love fills all hearts open and thirsty
For this Holy Spirit.

In all things is this love,
and in human kind, it was placed
In the safe keeping within the heart,
a sanctuary that is nurtured by love,
not to keep, rather to give away.

## The Tests of Loving Kindness

Often come when another misreads
this gracious act as weakness.
No backbone, they assume in their
ignorance, which speaks louder than words
ever could.

The one who practices loving kindness
would never point out misdeeds of others.
Overlooking the faults, where earthquakes
lie in wait to disrupt with abruptness,
the error of the ways,
they misunderstand kindness.

And so some blunder through life
judging other's behavior:
those with gentle hearts, living in grace
and profound kindness, as whoa, look, no backbone.
And wonder why they do not stand up for themselves;
put the ne'er-do-wells in their place.
Give them what for-- they ask for it,
just can't go round wearing one's heart on their sleeve.

Blinded in eye and heart of ever seeing the ones who:
choose love over power,
know God Will is Good Will,
whose strength comes from giving
whatever is needed at a moment's notice...

They find their attitudes have caught up with them
leaving them weathering the trail of tears so bitter
when Karma comes to collect its taxes to balance the
ledger of life.

Yes, those who judge actions of others
created by their small mindless minds,
stand charged in realization that they themselves have created
blunders against themselves.

For none can touch the hearts that stand strong,
no matter how toxic are the thoughtless forms
that shadow the way into the knowing,
which they may never know
until life teaches them better.

How sacred is choice?
How sacred is withstanding the
Tests of loving kindness?

## The True Artist of Life

The true Artist of Life,
draws upon the spiritual resources
from the source of All that IS,
for All is Love.

It is this which fine tunes consciousness
to purity of vibrational energy,
which plays the heart strings
made strong in the pool of creation.

We are conceived in like image of the Creator...
with the twin traits of creativity, receptivity,
conception, reception,
allowing each moment to be an opportunity
to BE more God-like.

And the best is, we are no longer
held captive by the Law of Opposites.
The Divine Polarity sings songs,
clearing the pull of negative forces,
so that Love Supreme can resonate within the Heart.
The Grace of God makes Truth abundantly clear.

All the blessings are Here Now
and Spirit lives within the true artist of life,
finding there is nothing left but to serve
God among the human race,
serving all life,
with Divine Unconditional Love.

# The Unrecognized Spiritual Law of Absurdity

How does the law of absurdity manifest in my life?
Well, let's take a look at life being a random walk
in the parking lot of life, with no spaces
unless one has a handicap sticker, or, oh yes,
now there is a space for pregnant women
that's what the sign says.
Thank you for that clarification.

And what about advertisement, stating Live Music!
Does that mean it is not dead music?
I can see it now...Tonight's Venue, Live Music
with the Grateful Dead...

My tire goes flat, in fact two blow out.
My trunk is the place where nothing can be found.
Yet look anyway for a jack and a spare.
Don't find a jack, and the spare is flat, but
the good new is, I found a large can of tuna
missing since who knows when.

When I lost my mind, it was such a relief.
I did not go looking for where it might be
but darn, if my mind did not find me
and it was singing "O lonesome me!"

I feed the dog some yummy turkey
and the dog runs behind me to trip me
as I turn, and guess what, ouch
I fell over the dog,

and broke my shoulder.
What did I learn from this?
How much a broken shoulder hurts?
And how to sleep sitting up if and
when sleep comes, before it is time to get up
and face another day
learning from the Law of Absurdity.
The list goes on and on, like when
I am so exhausted I fall into bed
until grand daughter's screams jolt me awake
I run to the kitchen, to see flames
and smoke pouring out of the oven.

It seems she thought the pizza would warm quicker
In the card board box, with the thermostat on broil.
Quick thinking, I grab the sprayer from sink
open the oven with a flair, spray water to douse the flames
when I hear my grand daughter yell
Don't get my pizza wet!

I learn to laugh when the laughter comes.
I have even learned to laugh and cry at the same time.
I laugh at most things, but mostly at myself.
I keep myself entertained,
just a laugh a minute.
It is so absurd to know
I of myself do nothing, so let go let God
do the rest.
What's right with this picture
and why should I care?
That is what is so funny--I don't care
because I care too much.

I just go along singing a song,

walking with one of my great teachers,
talking The Law of Absurdity.
And deep inside I know, I know
for all intents and purposes,
I am a little crazy, a little weird.

God has plans for me, yes He does.
But He seems to have misplaced the blueprints.
So God's will be done,
If it all comes down to the stages of Life,
Then would it be filled with meaning, or meaningless?
Full or empty?

Change rearranges landscape of remembering.
What is important?
Invest in love.
Cherishing life brings experiences needed for developing
God qualities, and practice makes perfect, sort of...

Empty spoke to my heart today,
saying: Read fine print of your Golden Contract,
Do not become forgetful or complacent.
Remember, empty is good, because it can be filled,
and full is good, because it can be emptied.

Keep focused always on
the never-ending study of Consciousness,
filling the heart with truth and wonder.

I heard God speak to me today, He said I
AM a keeper.
Said I in reply "Thank you God, for keeping me, yet
may I ask, does one of your keepers also get to
keep something?"

God answered:

"Now that you ask the question, yes, as one of my keepers
you can be a Keeper of the Sacred Flame,
holding it high so it can light the way for Souls to find
what they are seeking."

I said: "Thank you God. It is always an honor and
a pleasure to serve you,

*For the slightest touch of your love within my heart*
*Is heaven to me.*

And yes, it is a tough job, but someone has to do it.

And so life goes on, from the ridiculous to the
sublime with

the ever present Law of Absurdity.

## The Searing Love

What is this love that sears my very being?
What is this love that melts my heart,
leaving only the beating rhythm,
searing, burning, in this yearning for God,
whose fiery light coldly burns all of me to ashes.

The wind of God blows all that is left, the
tattered and torn fragments of no thing.
The yearning, the learning, the searing love
leaves nothing in its wake, just the silence,
just the sacred nothing,
and the mirror of God reflects nothing of me or you,
just the image and likeness of God
whose song is the silence,
is the stillness,
is of the music of God.

Leaving only consciousness of being, of living,
of serving, of knowing
that this searing love burns away
all that is not of Itself,
leaving only all that we are in this moment of eternity:
A spark of God with the power of love, to ignite,
to arouse a love for God in others.
Just for Love
This Searing Love.

# A True Story, This Is

Through Jazz and Blues
I heard your voice,
And in its rhythms,
I heard your heartbeat.
Soul took flight on the notes,
As on sound waves they traveled
into the sacred night.

I was listening to the sounds of the night,
when in the distance I heard a Song
of Soul, the sound of love and despair
wrapped into blues chords traveling the night air.

Seeking to find the source of this lament,
so beautiful it drew me down quiet streets
to a bar.
And opening the door I entered
To find no one there, save for the barkeep
and a blues guitarist playing his heart instrument
with all the love of Soul.

Our eyes met.
He knew why I had come.
Transfixed, I listened as
this music washes Soul clean.
With tears streaming down my face
we smiled, I nodded my head,
And closed the door behind me.

The notes followed me home,
and forever that Soul, whose name I did not know,
and I were bonded in the music of God.
For I had no doubt that,
that night I saw and heard God
playing blues guitar in a lonely bar
Just for me.

# Soul Memory

The sheer ecstasy of nothing in all the universes
can compare, nor would I wish to compare
the incomparable experiences stirring deep within Soul:
How to begin?

Here it is: A near, yet distant memory of Me, Soul,
existing on a lonely outpost, somewhere
out in the vast galaxy.
I waited; it seemed like eons of time.
The loneliness of deep space always embraced me
and I waited,
wondering what I was doing here, and what was I to do,
while here.

While I waited, and watched, I thought,
perhaps I am the watcher.
Maybe this is what I am here to do,
just watch asteroids play, and stars being born,
mourning deaths of stars.
I had a great view of the galaxies and constellations,
the universe moving in
rhythm with the eternal deep stillness.

After eons passed, I began having visitors--
they said they were dropping in to check up on me.
As we began to communicate,
I discovered they were Spiritual Masters
of the Highest Order.
They disclosed they would be coming to teach me
the secrets beyond matter, energy, time, space.

At this time I was formless, yet conscious of being.
I could see all the worlds at a glance,
I knew I was part of what I saw,
the very fabric of this substance of space.
What did I learn?

I was instructed to pay close attention to the comings
and goings of the planets as they orbit around the sun;
to study how gravity worked,
and how it sustained the conditions for life.
I had no needs or wants; I did not need sustenance.

After eons it seemed, something stirred within me,
a feeling of anticipation,
of looking forward to the visits of the Masters.
Once they ask me to listen to the soundless sound,
the music in its pure, formless whisper,
of the turning of a star.

Is all this a distant memory, embedded within
Soul experience?
As I recall the deep well of learning,
I will always know the immensity
of the Universes of God's love.
Was I an asteroid? Or am I but a speck, a cell in the
Consciousness of God?

I have no answers.
I know my home is not this world,
I am in this world
But not of it.
Does any of this bring me closer
into the very heart of God?

Can't say.
What I comprehend within me is the deepest,
most sacred, holy silence,
leaving me almost not wanting to breathe,
because this would shatter the silence
whose sound swallows me whole.

I am digested in the sound.
Distilled in the art of nothing much,
a distant star waiting to be born,
an asteroid out in space where the only light
in this lonely vigil was star light,
a cell within the body of God
waiting, waiting, waiting,

and now I am one Soul Rising.

## What Is True Surrender?

I find myself entering this moment with randomity
as a guide, for the depth of understanding stands on
illusive ground, ever changing as cloud formations
painted by wind, blowing away like drifts of snow
crystal clear on a winter's day.

The inner hush, so overwhelming, attempts escape
through the door of consciousness as the heart seeks
a responding truth in answer to this most sacred question,
What is True Surrender?

When do I feel most surrendered?
For starters, when I keep my daily appointment with
the Beloved at the Temple within.
This is the timeless moment,
when the Beloved listens to my heart,
and adjusts my Sound and eternal rhythm so it is
in tune with life, giving me the spiritual
stamina to meet the day with a loving heart,
that can listen to the call of Spirit and
respond when I am called to serve.

Service is also another way to stay surrendered.
For as I walk every day in a state of Grace,
to shine with the love of God, as it flows through me
to touch all that I meet, let me be, let me see
through the eyes of the Beloved, then
each moment exists unchanged.

Yet, what is True Surrender?
Maybe it is all the little moments of surrendering
that are deposited in a Spiritual bank account
and each successful surrendering moment adds up.

Then again perhaps it is an attitude, a state of
consciousness, combined, entwined, and woven
into the fabric of being...so Soul moves through
life living in a Surrendered State.

Would it be accurate to say,
no matter what happens around Soul, even if
the walls of all known existence come falling down,
the God-given ability to be centered in Spirit each moment
would inclusively mean, a heart committed to a
Surrendered state.
Is God's will be done, here and now
as it is always in the heavenly worlds?

To abide in Spirit forever requires an all of me commitment.
So what is True Surrender?
A complete unwavering acceptance of all that comes.
And the only action is no reaction, just
love in all its glory, just gratitude for all the
gifts the Beloved brings to Soul.

With gratitude, loving acceptance,
And appreciation, does the heart open to receive
God Love?
For only does Soul in purity and grace,
find that true surrender is the giving in of all things,
not the giving up, for that would be nothing.

The giving in love, and service, is the state
of true surrender understood and embraced.
Why? Because Soul knows without the Beloved
and the Creator, It is nothing, nothing,
for Soul lives, moves, and has Its being within
the giving in, true surrender.

This is all Soul can do: exist and know God Love,
for Soul is the fuel, the glue that sustains it
in all the worlds of God, from the edge of eternity.
The way of the eternal is the way a Soul comes into
realization of all of what is true surrender.
So again I ask, What Is True Surrender?

When I contemplate this question,
even my heart skips a beat.
For in the realms of blessed consideration,
it seems this is one of the most
scared of questions Soul could ever ask
of the Creator.

Is it complete acceptance of all life
that brings me the experience of learning more
about maintaining a loving attitude
no matter what comes?

Is it staying balanced no matter which way
the wind blows, or the rivers flow?
I love life, I love living, I love Loving.
Life is precious to me,
and loving service is what I do.
And so if there is a choice as to what to do,
I surrender my will to you forever.
I abide in your loving presence, why would I ever

choose to leave you Beloved?
I want to stay, to serve God by serving and loving all life.
Yet I am surrendered to being here and now
for in this moment,
The Beloved takes my hand.

## To Know Love in Its Entirety

Powerful truth, the call of Love...
To give love, to receive love,
is so powerful.
Soul is drawn like moth to flame.

What can I ever know of love,
the love that is unwavering?
that can dive into the depths
of the ocean of love and mercy,
that can stand before the Angel of Love,
that can see love in its entirety,
and feel the searing love
burn away all the bones left in the dust
that sincerity brings as a guest.
Love is, all is love.

Yet this means nothing in the face of the overwhelming vastness of
the knower, the known,
and yet, still unknown.
This face of love
hides from my understanding,
and when I reach out my arms to embrace Its Allness,
I am left with nothing there.
Smoke and mirrors water and fire
dance beyond the flames of invisible reality,
laughing at the tricks being played in this place that
displaces me.

Yet I care not, I am a fool for God, being drawn into
where this overwhelming love
leaves me in anguish,
as this cry of despair leaves my heart.
My Heart has emptied itself of tears.

How can I know love in its entirety, even with all the
melting experiences given in golden dreams?
Yet the memory of this love fades; is this love?
The love I know exists beyond the horizon,
the love of which I do not have a clue,
the love beyond this grasp of being,
leaves me humbled, grateful,
to be content with what little thimbleful of its vastness
I have been allowed to taste.
Is IT beyond all comprehension, this Love?
How could I, a mere speck within the consciousness
of God, know anything outside itself?

If this is the key, where is the lock?
Can the whole of love, all the secrets of love be contained
within a speck of itself?
I can't say, yet the relentlessness of my longing
will not allow me to stop.
Does it come down to vision, or is it hearing, or comprehension, or
nothing at all
that will allow a speck of itself to know
the whole of itself?

How can cosmic dust, the ingredient of star formation,
know of all the galaxies and constellations in all the universes
of which it is a part?
Yet, consider, the speck, the itty bitty grain of sand,
forgetting the desert from whence it came,

forgetting the shore where the ocean waves wash away
its memory of place, desert or the oceans roar,
upon the sands of time.

How crushing this blow of never,
never knowing the interval of changes
between a single heart beat to behold this searing love?
All I can see is the aftermath, the residue left behind,
the utter loneliness before me, at dawn's early light.
I am desolate in my sincerity,
Angel of Love, why do you haunt me?
This face of love, of which one glimpse I was given,
changed me forever,
leaving me yearning for the All of It.
Yet this Love I seek,
chases me as I chase It,
playing hide and seek with my heart as the playground.
Perhaps it is so simple; I am missing what is right in front of my eye.

An Inner voice whispers to me:
Stop looking, seeking, searching, for what is the all in all.
Step back: See what you have been looking for.
Can you see the air you breathe in and out?
Yet you know air exists, how?
By its life sustaining presence.
Love is not a thing, a noun that can be found for someone to say,
I found IT!
If it cannot be found, how do we know love is real?
That it exists?
And Soul cries out I know! I Know.

In what ways can Soul know Love, this God Love?

As a presence?
How does a Presence make itself known?
Why am I moved to tears when I see the
hand of Spirit working its wonders in the world?
Is this The Love?
Not all notice the moving hand of Spirit at work.
Is its reality less, because of this, or am I seeing things?
No, only nouns are things, remember?
Love can only be experienced by a Soul, who grants
Love the freedom to enter the Open Heart, the one
willing to demonstrate God's Love for Soul,
willing to manifest God's Presence in this world.

Did I, Soul earn the right to be a converter of this
God Stuff?
No? I made a contractual agreement to do so, as a way to
thank you to Spirit for the gift of consciousness.

Wait! That's IT! The gift of consciousness!
This living, breathing, fluidity; the very substance,
the glue which restores Soul,
strengthening it, so it becomes fit to
receive the full measure of God Love!
Is it any wonder, as we look for Love, we discover,
it is not out there,
in place or out of place, lost or found.
It is in the Heart.

All we need do is give it away, so more Love can come in,
and with Love's transforming power,
we become magnets of love,
enlivened to give service within the worlds of God,
and man.

So would it suffice to say, Angel of Love,
You are my Heart?
You hold this heart so tenderly,
breathing life into it until it begins beating
on its own with love and purity.

And yet I say, I am barely scratching the surface...
To know love in its entirety.

## To Live in the State of Selflessness

What is this state of grace I am immersed in?
It leaves me breathless,
for I am gone in this feeling of complete freedom.

Sacred surrender holds me forever,
as a higher law I am given to abide by and
hold dear in the temple of the heart.
Just let me be, let me see, through the eyes
of the Beloved One.

Yes, there is much to be done
to strengthen Soul's awareness of its Divine nature,
as more is required of every Soul.
Love yourself, trust yourself,
to finally know beyond all knowing,
how loved you are.

The sweet softness of gentle raindrops condensed
from the river of life
falls into a thirsty heart, the lonely heart,
whose loneliness seems to eat Soul alive,
revealing there are no more questions,
just the Quest, feeding this desire that consumes Soul
in its longing for God.

Knowing nothing is as real as this moment,
and this relentless pulling and pushing of Soul
beyond all limitations illusion gives,
for you to play make believe.

You know of which I speak:
"when I am more perfect,
"when I have a compassionate heart
"when I know more,
"when I know more...more, more, more."

And the distance from the goal becomes farther away;
the agony intensifies.
Why do we do what we do to forget
the greatness of Soul, the recurrent belief
that you,
and you, and you, are not worthy.

How can this be? Why is this belief so embraced
by those who know better?...
those who have kissed the hem of the Lord's robe,
and had the kiss returned.
This belief is like a virus, short circuiting
the Spiritual dynamics.
Let the burning begin again,
so truth can reveal itself in the ashes.

This is just a perception of this sad state of affairs,
when Soul turns from Its radiance, losing the way, falling
into belief of unworthiness.
When this happens, they are basically saying
they know better than God,
better than the Beloved.
What false humility! It could choke a horse.
It is Spiritual arrogance.

In a heartbeat, turn around, see that your flaws,
your weaknesses, matter not to the Beloved.
Why you may ask?

Because Soul is called to serve,
not from its strength, but from Its weakness.
Called to love, to give selflessly each moment.
What is more thrilling than the touch of God's hand
upon thy brow?

This is the melting love, that brings selflessness
to the heart,
and in the silent marriage of desire and feeling
and longing,
Soul surrenders all pretense, embraces non perfection
as a Spiritual law, passing this test.
So now Soul can just get on, with lightening speed,
its simple mission: to give and receive Divine love,
to henceforth live in the state of selflessness

## Truth Catchers

What moments in life become truth catchers?
Is it the moments that come crashing
into the consciousness like a symphony
playing a huge crescendo,
big banging Soulful sound to beat the band in ragtime
with all the fanfare, whatever the moment is.

However truth also comes on silent feet,
and quicker than a wink or a blink it is gone.
The path is getting refined;
thin line between humility and humiliation.

For of a truth worthy of consideration, consider this:
the moment is now a foregone conclusion,
and only the residue left behind within the chambers
of the heart, are put to the test of what is real for you.

Truth stands alone, has no opposites.
Majestic in its relationship to Spirit,
it serves as an awakener for truth seekers,
those whose desire is to know
what is real, what is true, what is the way to discover
the answers deep inside.

Yet within the great unknown, as Soul journeys from
incarnation to incarnation and discovers
something is missing, how does one go about
finding this something?
This is the point in the journey where

relentlessness and fierce determination
consumes Soul to know that only
the heart can see what the blinded eye cannot.

Love and love alone can answer all questions.
Love can heal all the wounds of an aching heart.
And truth, what is truth? It is only what resonates deep
within the chordal structure of beingness,
inside, where Spirit resides,
where Spirit carries on the dictates of God,
with or without one's conscious awareness.

So the old adage of what you are looking for is
what is looking for you,
takes on new meaning.
Truth becomes a reality and
love becomes the beingness of Soul.
When Soul is free from the control
of the mind, it can embrace this simple truth.

What is truth?
Is there a difference between your life and life itself?
Truth relative, and absolute, holographically speaking,
is still what's true for you according to your own light,
your own understanding, based on your own experiences.

And why is this?
Maybe because love is all there is,
because God is Love, and
this is what makes this lifetime journey so awesome.

What is important? Trust.
Trust and honor Spirit within each Soul.
Listen to their stories of truth as they

have experienced it.
Value their journey. Remember, if your journey
has been difficult, so is the journey for every Soul.

If you have the gift of your truth, your ability and
capacity to love, give it away, for it isn't yours
until you do.

So what is truth, and how does one's Truth catcher work?
I don't know; however I do know love,
and I do recognize the blessings in my life,
and am filled with compassion and gratitude,
in knowing God loves me.

I feel compelled to pass it along,
wherever Spirit directs...
What else is there to do with the gifts of Spirit?

## What Happens When the Wait is Over?

Depends on the interpretation or perception of wait.
Let's see some of the possibilities:
I wait,
I am waiting,
for what?
What for?

If the wait is over, what are you waiting for?
Waiting teaches patience for sure.
Waiting is difficult when one is in a hurry
Waiting is endless if one does not dwell
in the present moment.
Boredom sets in when the illusion of nothing to do
takes over without a moment's notice.
How can there ever be nothing to do?
The greatest design of the human body is hands--
consider hands.
All they do to serve you in this world,
they were meant for far more than just twiddling
the thumbs.

A handful of wisdom to consider is all the ways
we find ourselves waiting...
to give birth waits for conception,
the embryo waits for pregnant development,
waits for labor and delivery, the baby waits for nourishment
waits for the one to nurture.

Unforeseen circumstances may keep us waiting,

so hurry up and wait, just wait until you grow up.
Wait until you have kids, you just wait, wait, wait....
for planes, trains, buses,
something to open, close, sunrise, sunset,
waiting for love, for the right one to come along.

Yes it seems we do a lot of waiting
in this lifetime journey: waiting to be born, to die,
to live, and here in the nick of time
which waits for no one.
It goes on endlessly...

Perhaps there is another consideration:
creative use of time, in the moment
through quiet transformation of time to rhythm changes.
Soul got rhythm, who could ask for anything more
or less, and so life goes on and on
depending on how we wait.

Within, the seeds of patience grow and life
teaches us different concepts of waiting.
Wait changes into service!
"I wait on thee O Lord, Do what you will with me."
Here is a news flash: there is no waiting when
one embraces the path of service.
It is all in God's time, which is timeless.
And then a thought, unbidden, whispers,
*I wonder how long I have kept God waiting?*

Yet, no matter, when the sacred moment awakens Soul
to the conscious realization that revitalizes,
and transformation gives birth to the song of life,
singing within of a Presence,
a presence awaiting Soul to make way, to welcome

the thrilling presence of the Beloved.
For now it enters into the very fabric of our being,
fulfilling our life in ways unforeseen,
until patience and surrender open the door of
consciousness, revealing golden moments of service,
endless opportunities for Spiritual growth.

All I need to know in this moment, is that I am exactly where Spirit
needs me, and all is in perfect accord with God's Divine plan,
just for me...Soul.

Did the imperfect concept of the waiting game change?
No, that illusion is still lurking like a spider web waiting to
catch one unawares, into its snare, in a heart beat
if we become forgetful to remember Soul is free
from the playground of the Mind.

Soul, through experience, knows that the beauty is
even if we forget,
the moment we catch ourselves,
we free ourselves, liberated in the moment.

Soul is never held captive because of its mistakes.
When awareness awakens Soul to its truth and
learns something new in this Now,
Time waits for no one, Love endures forever,
love is timeless.

When the wait is over, true service begins.
There is no waiting on holy ground.

# When Did I Know God Loves Me?

Was it as a young child on a summer day,
lying on pine needles, looking up through branches
of a tree, seeing the blue sky, as birds sang nearby,
feeling the warmth of the sun on my skin,
and a sense of peace filled my heart, knowing all is
right with the world?

Was it at night when saying my prayers before sleep,
and a feeling of love embraced me, instilling trust
that I would awaken in the morning to a new day,
to laugh and sing and play in this world anew?

Was it the first time my heart was broken
and I felt like I was dying from a pain that
took my breath away, yet falling into a restless sleep,
to awaken with the morning light, still alive and
knowing I won't die of a broken heart?

I discovered the gift of learning from the pain,
yes, learning insights about God's grace,
and how God's love sustains me, even in my darkest hour,
showing me I am never ever alone.

I came to know myself under all circumstances,
which were sacred gifts from God, giving me
many opportunities to develop courage, compassion,
and a loving heart, knowing 'tis better to give than receive,
so that in God's time I would learn the secret
of my own Divinity.

How?
Through realizing that giving and receiving are
two sides to one golden coin,
for I must be open to the reception of Divine Love
to enter my heart, uncompromised,
for the purpose of giving it all away.
That the only love I have is the love I give away...
yet my cup runneth over.

The spiritual laws of life and living are so fine tuned
to the greatest of all laws—Love.
The fulfilling of this law is why I live,
and why the world needs God in its life.

Each of us, as we grow and learn, finds truth
in listening to how God speaks to us each moment,
and giving back to life in Service...
for lo and behold, we do not have to prove God exists.
We need only to manifest Its Presence in this world
through our actions, which always speak louder that words.

So when did I know beyond all knowing, beyond all doubt,
God Loves Me?
Was it when I learned to love myself as God loves me?
Was it when I learned to choose words carefully, to bring
peace to others?
Was it when I knew that how I treat others tells more
about the condition of my heart?
Was it when I learned to serve all life as a way to say
thank you God for giving me this life,
to love and serve You and the Beloved?

All I know is I live, move, breathe, and have my being
in your presence,

and it is by your grace I *am* your Humble Servant.
Thank you with love,
for showing me the way into your Kingdom.

So with Love, may I ask
When did you know?

## Voluntary Incarceration

To what do I owe this honor?
Why was I selected to experience this
contemplative journey?
Sometimes there are no answers to the ways Spirit
works in the life of Soul.

I will attempt to record this journey as best I can,
although the challenge is great in bringing
what happens in the inner worlds, to this plane of existence,
and in vain try to dress them
in words that are fitting in this world,
for clarity and understanding.

I began my journey this night by sitting in
silence, placing my attention on my Beloved Master,
and softly began singing HU,
a love song to God.

Now I am in an unfamiliar place, and it is made
known to me that I am waiting for a limo to take me
to my assignment this night.

The limo arrives, and as I enter the vehicle, I am aware
the Beloved is here, and will escort me personally.
What I was embarking on with this assignment, I am told,
would need my agreement, and my loving,
willing, commitment.

This service, would be nothing less than voluntary

Incarceration.
Without hesitation, I agreed.
We arrived at the destination, and with blessings
from the Beloved, I got out of the limo.
A guide appeared.

There was before me, a mountain, a great mountain.
Is this, I wondered, The Mountain of God?
I could hear it calling my name, and the desire to
answer this call was overpowering, yet before
I responded, I decided to take in my surroundings.
I needed to know more about this voluntary incarceration
and what was required of me, and to what, I had agreed,
hoping I would have what was necessary to fulfill this
task the Beloved had ask me to do.

There were two paths up to the top of this great Mountain:
one was very winding and indirect, the other path went
straight up the mountain to the very pinnacle.

At the foot of this mighty Mountain,
was a dilapidated shack.
I was told this would be my shelter should I have need of it. As I
looked around the inside of the shack,
I could see through the sides of it.
The wind blew through cracks of rotted wood
that made the walls.
There was a wooden plank or two nailed to a wooden rise that made
a bed, that would not be conducive to sleep,
I thought.
I hope I will have no need for this shelter.

Then through the translucent mist I saw several temple-
like structures.

As I looked closer, I saw much activity.
There were people dressed in all styles,
from all walks of life, entering these structures
and forming themselves into groups.

I got the feeling the groups were prearranged,
by agreement.
As the activity ceased, in an orderly manner,
each found where they were to be seated.
There were groups of twelve seated in circles.

Each group was given a task; they were required to find
a harmonic solution, and whatever the solution would be,
it would require all hearts to be engaged
in loving agreement for the outcome.
I also got the feeling that each task, given to each group,
was of utmost importance for their continuing service
in the world of man.

Even though every Soul within these circles was from different
parts of the world of man,
whatever the solution arrived at would be a vital seed to assist Souls
in need of spiritual gifts, enabling greater endurance required for
the tests to come.
For when the tests come, Souls must be prepared.
I thought these Souls gathered here, in this place
were to be the carriers of these vital seeds.

It seemed I was invisible to those in this gathering.

Everyone was aware of the deep Spiritual significance
of what was required of them,
while I was still wondering why I was there.

As I walked around, listening and observing, I began
to notice something astounding to me.
Whatever their task and challenge was,
as they discussed it I could see the answer, and
as I gently held the solution in my consciousness,
members of a group would catch it.

Then I would move on to observe another group,
and repeat the task, and again, the various groups
that caught the solution to restore what Spirit needed
through their harmonious resolution,
to their specific challenge, they would know then they
were free to leave, and return to the world of man,
to fulfill their mission.
When one group left, other groups replaced them.
Though no group had the same challenge,
how they were required to respond was the same.
It seemed time passed, except in this place
there was no time.

At one point, there was an intermission,
so I decided to explore.
The presence of the mountain was overwhelming.
No matter where one went, the sound of the mountain
calling seemed to overshadow everything.
But it did not matter to me,
for I somehow knew the mountain knew my name
and would not forget me.
It was clear to me I was not here to climb the mountain
this time, for the mountain would always be here.

In my continued exploration of this place, I found
a court yard in between two of the temple-like structures.

It was an obstacle course with all kinds of endurance exercise
programs, set up for traveling Souls, to come
here and enter into this special training program.
In so doing they became stronger and stronger in preparation for
the next step on their journey home to God.

The interlude of rest was over and I returned to my task.
I was interested only in serving in the way
Spirit directed me when I arrived.
This was where I felt great urgency, and I felt how
imperative this task was for the spiritual survival
of this mission these Souls were here to do.
They were fulfilling an agreement;
my interest was in assisting them in their mission.

It was not running the obstacle course,
nor resting in the shack, and not climbing the mountain
as it called me by name.

So for now in this moment I was serving
in this outpost somewhere beyond time and space.
I am serving a life sentence, voluntary incarceration.

What this experience was about, I don't have a clue.
The old saying that comes to mind fits:
"Ours is not to reason why, ours is but to do or die."

## How One Finds the Way to Loving Kindness

How does one learn kindness? Consideration?
Perhaps by being treated unkindly a few times
and we cry 'uncle.'
Or perhaps we savor the feeling
of hurts that deeply go to the quick, and say
*Let me remember this, let me not forget this,*
*so I will never treat another Soul in this way, ever.*

Learning anything of lasting value
that uplifts the whole of mankind,
must require knowing what something is--
so deeply, so totally, the pain forever a burning memory,
calling Soul to discipline itself
in how it responds to others
with responsibility always, and yes,
self sacrifice becomes as natural as
breathing away any diminishing of others,
for to do so would surely diminish self as well.

All things manifest in Soul's garden of delight.

When grace prevails like a sweet kiss upon the cheek of
a sleeping child, dreaming in all innocence with total trust
that it will awake from sleep and see love as its eyes open
to that blessed place where Soul dwells
in the love, cuddled within its surety of trusting
all things in its world.

Innocence prevails even when pin pricks of living

poke holes within the experience of harshness
required for Soul to know, and to choose,
when life gives you a doubled-edged sword,
to not let power wield the sword to wound,
but to let love have its way of gentleness and healing,

Yes, give the living gift of peace and contentment,
showing the way to increase beyond measure,
the learning way, and the teaching way, as they join
forces with the only way to learn, is with love,
through our own choice, then knowing all
experiences accelerate the growth and knowing.

Through all of the acts of unkindness, inconsideration and
slights, that become our teachers, and what are they
teaching us? Compassion, for starters, and a vow
to treat others kindly, justly, with loving consideration,
striving to always inspire others to keep the heart open.

I have heard it said nothing is worth it if
one Soul must be sacrificed to gain it.
As I have experienced life, this holds true for me.

Weep if you must, for tears are important.
They wash the eyes so one can see the grace of God,
so when acts of unkindness are gifted to you by
thoughtless people, blinded by ego,
remember, within this teaching moment of hurt,
you get full blown understanding why
you must give your best with Love, and always be kind.

As Soul grows stronger and has courage to
examine one's own intentions, gained the hard way,
through all of the slings and arrows that

intentionally were acts of unkindness,
it is found that Spiritual maturity is gaining a foothold
within the temple of the heart, bringing peace
and contentment.

And so the blessings come
with great abundance as you surrender with love.
And Contemplation brings a smile upon your Heart,
and your eyes fill with appreciation, for it is discovered
appreciation is contemplation,
and patience is your reward, and perhaps
the best blessing of all the learning is
the knowing that you are truly one of a kind,
outside the box, when there is no longer a box.

You have withstood the storms that assaulted
you without retaliation, and now you swim
within the ocean of Love and Mercy forever.
For me, this was how I found the way to Loving Kindness.

## I Remember

Was it a Spring day in May?
Soft and hazy, preparing for the summer solstice?
I can't say
because I hadn't as yet arrived on the scene.
The scene? A quiet city block in the Atlanta suburbs.
It was a peaceful day, ordinary, people going
about their lives, lost in thought, or lost, or found.

No one aware of a most unusual occurrence,
one that would happen so silently no one
would be the wiser.
Yet for me it would be a profound experience.
What am I talking about?

In this quiet neighborhood scene,
a mother is walking up the sidewalk toward the house
she called home,
perhaps musing about her life...perhaps,
or her 11-month old daughter, her firstborn,
or her second pregnancy, which would be due in August.

A women who is taking care of a baby, is anxiously
awaiting the return of its mother, picks up the baby
and walks out onto the second story porch;
leaning over the railing, looking to see if the
mother approaches.

The mother sees her looking, and perhaps she waves,
perhaps the baby sitter waves in turn.

An ordinary moment of serenity turns
the next few seconds into horrifying despair,
as the baby falls from the baby sitter's arms,
and crashes to the ground below.
Time stands still.

This is where I came in.
Who am I?
I am Soul, the one chosen
to walk into this baby body.

This is the story of my arrival onto the scene
that day in May.
You may scoff, or in disbelief shake your head, but if
you are patient, I will reveal to you how this came to be.

Being Soul, I was on the Soul Plane,
(the true home of All Souls, who are between Lives).
I was attending one of the classes available in
one of the many learning centers of Golden Wisdom.
I was immersed in my studies
when two Spiritual Masters approached me.
After greeting me, they let me know the reason
for their visit, they informed me that is was
now time for me to return to the Earth World to
continue my education.

I have always known my purpose and mission as Soul,
is to be trained in developing spiritual skills
so I may be an example of God Love in this world,
by being of Service to All Life.
They ask me if I was ready,
I was happy to say Yes!
They said, now let us go, we have found
the perfect body for you.

Escorted by these Spiritual Masters, we traveled
through a corridor of light and sound, into the
aforementioned scene
just in time to observe the baby falling,
the mother running and screaming, the baby sitter yelling
and screaming, the body falling to the ground,
neighbors running, dogs barking, peace shattered,
as was the baby's right leg above the knee—
two compound fractures.
Into this moment, I arrived.

I was instructed by the two Masters to enter the baby body,
as the Soul who inhabited this body was leaving.
Being true to my nature, I had a few questions,
such as, *Are you sure? Are you sure this is the 'right' body?*
*It's broken!*
They replied in unison, *Yes, this is the one, get in.*

*Okay,* I said. *But just tell me, will it be fun?*
They replied yes, it will be a lifetime
filled with laughter and tears; it will be fun.

Before taking their leave, they gave me a parting gift
of three directives:
*Always Remember, you must maintain your individuality,*
*and never believe anything until you can prove it*
*for yourself.*
*Always be true to yourself, and follow your heart.*
*If you do these three things you will leave this lifetime*
*with a higher state of consciousness than*
*you came in with."*

So into this baby's body I went;
I had arrived on the scene.

## *Warrior Soul*

In thoughts of you,
In recognition of you,
In seeing within your heart
the struggle to compromise,
To give an inch, life takes a mile or two.

In the splendor of you,
you still retain the majesty of wisdom
gained and regained from the ancient days.
Yes, it is still there burning, glowing, growing by leaps and bounds
igniting the worlds within and beyond with sacred flames
of love's refrain,
singing without fear of the notes,
expressions of God's voice piercing the
night of a long day. And your heart song keeps the light of
direction glowing, lighting the way
for those seeking the Way Shower.

As I pause and reflect your beauty,
tears magnify your greatness.
How honored am I for this gift of sight
that allows me to see you rise to
all challenges that come into your testing ground.
 I see you draw on the strength
learned in the lifetimes when your weaknesses
became your greatest teachers.

You are so dear and near as you walk the talk
embracing all that you are, with such tenderness,

weaving your self-hood, and God-hood
into your fabric of a living breathing no-holds barred

gentleness from beyond the stars embedded within
your original intent,
fulfilling itself in wondrous ways.

And you, in purity, wield a sword with great dignity
and honor, with more than a silent song of longing, to freedom
ringing in the ears of forever.

How blessed are the Souls that are assigned to you!
For your presence uplifts those who stand in your light
and does not limit their light, as you demonstrate how
they too find their own switch,
turning on their own qualities of illumination.
And one by one they experience their own greatness.

Yes I am blessed to see you, and with far-seeing insight
I smile, for once again we have met.
I celebrate and rejoice in this knowingness of you,
Warrior Soul.

## What Gets Your Attention?

Sweetness and light, yet bittersweet,
its tartness compresses the agreements made.

Yet all of it falls apart in the face of fear,
paralyzing consciousness,
getting a stranglehold on truth, on love.

How honest can we be?
How ruthless must we be?
What brutal honesty does it take to find truth,
Truth, which lies in one's own experiences,
not in the words of others.

It seems all love is erased without a moment's notice,
when fear flies in on empty wings.
Clipped wings fetter truth and honesty,
and without love, one can go no farther.

It is like trying to spit watermelon seeds
into the wind,
and the observer, the silent listeners,
have found waking up is hard to do.

It is broadcast to the four winds and the seven seas.
Stay tuned for the coming attractions
driven by distractions not ready or
willing to give up.

Forgetting what experience teaches Soul,
begging the question, "Which is best?"
A wandering Soul?
Or a heart at rest?

What keeps Soul going in spite of Itself?
How can Soul discern fiction from non-fiction?
What is true, what is real?
Must it be moon-glow?
And even if it is,
even for a fleeting moment, to see clearly
by the light of the silvery moon.

In the stillness shadows play hide and seek;
finders keepers, losers weepers
as rivers run wild.
Oh, child in the Wilderness,
bewildered, coming to terms with
the unity of chaos.

Soul knows, somewhere there is a place for us
to go, where golden bridges cross golden waters,
where golden sand cleanses the receptors
of Spirit, to behold,
a golden land of light and sound,
created from the fabric of dreams formed
through purity of service forever.

Thy kingdom come,
so come on, this is where you are to be,
to love, to serve, yes, here, within this golden land
of opportunity.

A spiritual gold rush, a gold mine,
not to be undermined
in this land of the Golden HU
where Service is supreme.

What gets your attention?

## Just Wondering 'bout Illusion

In this world of super-packed illusion,
What is Reality?
We find ourselves asking, Is this real? Is that Real?
Would true reality please stand up.

Sometimes you pick an experience on faith and hope,
using the mantra,
"Please, please, let this be real,"
even, even, even though
you know
deep down you know
even when mind tries convincing your better judgment otherwise,
the reality is,
when we listen, we know
what's real.

Love and love alone is real;
all else is illusion.
Soul must accept and live within Its own Divinity,
to rise out of the confusion of illusion,
as a champion of Divine Love.

## What Is Beyond Your Next Breath?

Just contemplating on what really matters in life,
in the moment, this moment.

With all the experience I have in all the worlds of God,
with all the insights, questions, answers, understanding,
understood, knowing what is the right thing to do,
to do the right thing, and realizing what is important,
for me it comes down or up to this:

If you love your cats, dogs, all animals,
your children, your mother, father, all the people
who mean anything to you, those who have touched
your life in any way throughout your journey,

love them, show them you love them, not just in words,
but in every way you live, move and think and feel
and even breathe.
Every thing you are must vibrate this universal
harmony of love in each moment.
For of a truth, this is all there is.
This moment: to love, to be, to give all that you are.

To make a statement to all life what you believe
you are, is nothing unless you live it.
We are only as good as this moment.

Yesterday, this morning, or any of the past moments
you have experienced, that have moved into the

hall of stored memories, there to recall...
do they bring you credibility this moment?
Do they count for anything?

Priceless memories are not worth much unless this
moment is fully accounted for NOW,
and you can answer the question,
"Did you put the power and love of Soul into each moment as you
have lived it?
What have you learned?

## Is There More to Be Said?

What more can be said about the heart
broken or healed through love and the loss of love,
which is illusion,
for love is never lost, but always here,
waiting to be recognized in all its glorious splendor.

We learn to see through the pain, the anguish,
that causes tears to fall like rain,
yet what more can be said
about these necessary experiences
that cause one to take pause, to cry for a moment,
or for eternity, however deeply
the wounds of learning are perceived
through the cleverness of illusion.

Yes, I know heartache can sometimes
take the breath away.
But when morning comes, Soul has learned
one does not die of a broken heart.

Wonder of wonders, and Soul seeks ways to creatively express the
wonder of it "feels like dying" breath,
yet alive and well, with a story to tell.

Yes, so many songs, so many stories would not have been expressed
or shared
without these wounds of the heart.
Yet, more can be said perhaps about the continuity
of living, of finding ways to give of oneself,
for the continuum of life here and now.

To ask oneself, what keeps me present?
Is there more to say of all the learning gleaned
through joy and laughter, tears and sorrow?
Each Soul has many stories to share—
through music, art, novels, poems,
and just plain ordinary living.

Sometimes, just getting through a day calls for
heroic measures.
Sometimes just getting out of bed of a morning takes
every ounce of courage to face another day.

Yet, Soul perseveres one step at a time, and discovers
its greatness in the process.
How lovely is the realization: Soul is eternal,
has no beginning and no end.
We are all children of the Light and Sound of God.

And as we cherish the gift of life, and go through
the lessons of living, the greatest gift comes to Soul--
the gift of a compassionate heart, filled with understanding.

A heart that has withstood all the assaults to stunt its growth,
and prevent its growing into Spiritual maturity,
to stand with the Spiritual giants
ready and willing to assist other Souls
caught in the illusions
of despair, of forgetting the true nature of Soul.

Those whose lights have dimmed as they grow weary,
and say to God,
"Now I lay me down to sleep,
I pray thee God my Soul to keep,
And if I die before I wake..."

.....please, God, help me....

The Spiritual Giants are the first responders
in these moments,
for we have experienced all things and have learned to
give everything needed in the moment, in the name of Love.
We have gone to the edge and back many times,
(and over the edge a few times).

In speaking for myself, I have faced madness
in my longing for God,
demanding God to show Himself, or I was leaving.

That got a laugh, because there is nowhere to leave to,
nothing to do but weep and wail and wait, and find
that quitting is not an option.

The dawn brings an awakening to surrender my will,
to embrace the Holy light of Divinity within me, Soul,
and in the darkest hour, discover
I Am Soul, and I am worthy of God's Love.

Every difficult situation I found myself in
was teaching me compassion, and unconditional love,
and most of all in each and every experience,
God was telling me,
"I love you. You must learn these things of Spirit, and there is no
other way for Soul to learn except by experience."

And now here Soul is, maybe battered and bruised,
yet wiser and stronger, and confident It will face what is to come
with grace, God Willing.
So I ask, what more is there to say, or do, or be,
as Soul makes its way back home, knowing

with all the experiences, training, and unconditional love
showered upon It,
that when it finds itself home, in the Heart of the Ocean
of Love and Mercy,
that it will choose to return into the World of Man
to serve the Beloved wherever Spirit needs.

I Am Here
I Am Now
and forever abiding
in God's Love
Forever...
Do what you will with me.

# What Is The Wonder Of it All?

Questions of wonder
that fuel imagination,
compelling the heart to fly
beyond the boarders of heaven,
where Soul takes flight,
delighting in newness, renewing, reinventing itself
in joyful recognition of self discovery.

What are answers to questions unasked,
and far out is not far enough to go
the distance when there is nowhere to go,
for grace adorns this present moment.

Canadian geese majestic riding wind currents,
flap their wings and soar.
Yet, I beheld a moment when they decided
to walk across a busy roadway,
to the ire of drivers in a hurry to go
no place, someplace, so the ears could
hear only car horns honking.

Impatience won out and feathers flew.

How sad it was, and left me to wonder,
Why were they walking across the busy roadway,
when they have the gift of flight?

The answer came from within: *Why do you,*
*O Soul, walk, crawl, when you to can soar?*

*Why do you choose to turn from your radiance*
*When you carry the light of sixteen suns?*
*Yes, the light of understanding floods memory,*
*of all the times you 'settled' for less than your true worth,*
*placing limitations on your God-Given*
*abilities, your consciousness dressed in rags,*
*begging for insight as to why.*

Oh how quickly we forget in the world of Man.
Yes, we forget we are inheritors of the Kingdom,
standing at the gate, with keys in our hand,
locking ourselves out of our true home.

## *What's In Your Heart?*

Do you love the Spirit of God in You?
White eagles and black birds
ride the wind currents, staying current to their
own purpose true, in love's way.

On the razor's edge of consciousness
I raise the sword of divinity.
Sharpened with a feathered edge, it
remains ready, cutting strings of any
attachments tying one to the illusions.

Never, never caught in the gripping
talons of timeless expedience,
wielding the blade, not to put up
with put-upon airs,
not worth the effortless effort.

What is to be, is just all that you are
in your greatness as Soul:
Majestic, Prince or Pauper.
Or are you pampered to death with empty nothings
begging for what you already have?

Soul is tested and beaten by life again
and again, stretched, pulled in all directions
until you cry, "YES, GOD, I AM ALIVE!"

Listening, even with all the pulling out of me, the
stripping of all that existed in the unseen shadow
worlds that came when not paying attention, those sneaky
unwashed thoughts come clean, in the laundromat of Soul,
Now do you love the Spirit of God in You?

## Stop and Go Before You Go

How can one stop and go?
Is this a statement of fact?
And if you go, don't come back.
Keep going until you are gone for good.

Don't stop here unless you have
forgotten what you are looking for.
Seek and you shall find,
and it may not be what you were looking for.
As Wise men say,
What you are looking for is what is looking for you.

This matters little; Soul must use
the gifts of Spirit, without conditions.
Live in Holy appreciation for all life.
The sands of God Time blesses all things;
even grains of sand, have a scared space
in the worlds of God,
for each has the potential
to be stars shining bright above the
worlds so high like diamonds in the sky.

Starlight, Soul Bright, Soul sings out
claiming Its birthright,
to inherit the keys to the kingdom within.

I know, I know,
God is in the details, so don't stop.
Keep on going until the end of time
runs out the door before it closes.

So open the windows of the heart and
let compassion and gratitude go
dance with the wind currents sound
of life fulfilling itself through heavens gate.

And as always it is love alone that is real.

Embrace the love you are, wear this garment
so all know you take a stand in love.

Live it, breathe it, sing it, give it accept it,
this greatness of love is.

And again I say,
if you are looking to please God
you are a day late and a dollar short...
just understand this truth...all any Soul
needs do is manifest God's Presence in the world.

How awesome is this?

## What's on Your Plate?

What is today's menu?
What is Spirit cooking up
in the way of experiences?

Everyone has the right to be wrong or right
is only labeled by a subjective viewpoint
pointless nonetheless.
The less we know about more and more,
the more we know about less and less.

Or lest we forget it's not about us,
but did you learn something?
My bad that's good.
Why? Why not?

And so we go into the dark, sacred nightfall
not falling for the illusion of opposites
beating on the door unhinged.

I am not fooling,
What's on your plate?
Are you being served?
Are you serving food for
Souls hungry for God?
Yes, they think they want steak,
none the wiser, that one day
they may go from wanting meat
to wanting spiritual food.

Partaking of God's daily menu,
to give it all, all of me, I say
let nothing get the best of me.
I have a great appetite
when Spirit cooks up today's menu,
Using God's recipes of love
For this day.

I say cook me tender, because I am tough.
Cook me tender, because my goose is cooked,
Overdone, yet this can only be known
By experience.

Through taking a bite out of time.
So savor the meals cooked up by Spirit.
Eat your fill, serve others as you are being served.
Otherwise the indigestion of complacency
sets in, and we just grow fat and die.

## When, Where, and What For?

One may ask the reason
for the anguish that befalls the heart of understanding,
outstanding in the rain of tears,
torn up with misunderstanding
as water falling sings a simple refrain,
"You are all wet."

Yet, ours is not to wonder why,
ours is but to do or...cry.
Dry out in the crucible of the heart,
and foolish though the heart may be,
without rhyme or reason, the beat goes on and on,
running out of time, tuning in to purity of rhythm,
keep it swinging, swing low, sweet harmony
singing grace notes.

Soul singing the blues, low down blues,
let it all hang out, down and out,
telling Soul's story of survival.
Listen up all that can hear,
know you have suffered and rejoiced
in all the experiences necessary for Soul's growth.

And like the Phoenix, Soul rises from the ashes
left behind from pain and sorrow and joy,
gaining liberation, which must be won and re-won
each moment, no guarantees.

Each moment stands alone; it is all there is.
Just don't forget to breathe.
All things replicate the Law of Spirit,
without duality, inflow and outflow
in Divine Order.

So when considering when, where, and what for,
Don't let forgetfulness lead the way.
It is just an ordinary day in the life of Soul
fulfilling God's special plan for gaining
Mastership in this lifetime.

Through laughter and tears Soul is nurtured
and strengthened by all that is holy.
And the funny thing is, everything is holy,
whether we like it or not, and we don't have to like it,
or love it.

However, as Soul moves in grace,
it fulfills the law of Love,
finding the simplicity of Its mission.
Listen, just listen, as the Holy Ones say,
to Listen is to Love.

Are you listening?

## *When*


When all is clear,
clear as a teardrop
sliding down a cheek

When nothing is hidden from Truth
standing in Truth
knowing all is love
and simply put, God Is Love.

When standing strong in Spiritual clarity
Knowing you are Soul, a spark of God
Learning about, and living through
The choices made.

When you know
and accept the responsibility
to learn and grow from mistakes
for they are a bridge to developing compassion
opening the heart of consciousness
into your greatness as Soul.

When you are true to yourself
following your Heart Truth
You will know Truth.
Truth regained like an old friend
has come out of the shadows into the light,
Your light
Giving you strength to swim the sea of remembrance.

## And Where Does It Go?

Out like a light, in the dark of night,
breaking boundaries once upon a midnight dreary.
Weary is the state of edgewise and no back up,
so the spilling is leaking beyond bliss into the drain.

No stopping the unstoppable know-it-all
with blinders on, unwilling to seesaw in all directions
the unbecoming victims of hit and running
into hiding.
How easy to forget the wise adage,
Stop, Look, and Listen, before you step out
in direction of choice.

Unwasted motion within the application
of the Law of Economy.
Neither here nor there; all things pass away
lest you save for a rainy day,
if waiting for sunshine means
you're all wet past point of no return.

Yet with all this convoluted phrasing,
what is so amazing—
Soul is accompanied by Grace of God
and the rudiments of service are arranged the easy way
when there is no picking or choosing,
just effortless companionship,
Soul and the indwelling Spirit,
carrying forth the dictates of God's will in the moment,
unlike any other.

The way of the eternal charting its course,
delegating favorable conditions.
And the delegation of Spirit's representatives
of the highest order, those who know
the value of each Soul, and demonstrate this at all times, enlivening
those in their sphere of influence with Spiritual self confidence,
showing beauty is in the eye of the beholder, indeed.
And by their deeds others waken to Soul's possibilities
to give and receive Divine love.

This mighty band in glorious reunion with the Beloved One
dancing cheek to cheek...
the beginning, the heart of it all.
Make no mistake, unless you learn something.

And so it goes, as Soul earns the difference
in spite of, or because
on a sentimental journey with no reservations.

Without love it makes little difference
what one does or does not do.

## Wherever Life Leads Us, Wherever Death Takes Us

Wherever life leads us, leaves us to go
on into the living of all things beautiful,
wherever death takes us on its journey
through out eternity on eagles wings into the
Spiritual Light life giving of itself in death's portal.

Why, why do you think we experience death?
To get what is beyond the dreams of the living
over and over, birthing the ending back to
the beginning, where all things and nothing exists,
save love.

No, don't save the love, love can never be saved;
it gives itself away.
The great teacher dries your tears of sorrow,
tasting joy bittersweet.
Nothing is ever lost when we gain in understanding
of the allness beyond the sounding clarion call,
calling Soul to the journey.

Take what you have learned of Death and Dying
and employ the secrets learned in the wisdom pool of
Divinity sweet.
This entitles you to hold the keys to God's Kingdom.

Open your heart, keep it open, going where you
have never gone before,
beyond the light, into the dark night,
which gives birth to the Light and Sound.

Yes, the silent darkness where ALL things gestate.

Explore the sacred darkness,
which is the birthplace of Soul.
It springs forth, giving you the gift of discovering
what you have forgotten,
what fear erased from your memory,
the many times, whenever Soul departed the Womb of Life,
the Living water.

Remember this place where all secrets about life and death,
are contained in the place where wildness abides, untamed.

Here are the Masters with no name
for you to call out. Why?
For you are the One in universal stillness
where God's Love abides.

Have you ever heard the laughter of God?
When you do, all that has been forgotten is remembered,
the times beyond number spent in the Master's Presence.
He never left you.

And his voice speaks once again:
*I am always with you is true.*
*Why did you leave me?*
*You must keep me with you, through all your*
*birth and death journeys.*
*The Heart of Soul sings my song.*
*Develop the listening ear.*
*Listen, hear the prelude of celestial symphonies*
*dying to be heard,*
*over and over and over until Soul gets it.*

Unfragmented glorious sounding rhythms,

the vibrational Sound of Creation.
Can you feel it?
Can you hear it?
Do you know it?
Where All begins, never ending beyond birth and death.
Willows weep over necessary nothings,
Tears asunder the living truth,

I AM THAT, I AM.

## Where, Oh Where

Where does joy live?
Is there an address to pinpoint
its location? Its existence in time and space?
Beyond zip codes, bar codes, encoded
stating the price, not its worth.

Who will buy this wonderful feeling?
This joy that makes Its home in the Temple of the Heart.

Consecrated at the altar where tears run dry,
never knowing why.
And the House of Joy opens
Its doors and windows,
and the sound of laughter
is like rain falling softly—
a sweet kiss, to quench
parched thoughts and ideas
parading across the desert sand.

## *Who Knows...*

All that can ever be known?
Whatever all that is.

I don't know, says the Mind, haven't got a clue.
However, I can give you opinions,
and I love telling you what to do.
There is not much I don't know, just ask me.

And the Causal body says, "Well going by past experience,
I can tell you why, not how.
And it always seems there is much ado about nothing.
I see I really don't know much either."

And the Emotional body weighs in with its report:
"Well, all things here I feel, are alive and well,
or not so well. I mean the Heart keeps breaking,
aching away.
It is a good thing Love is the spiritual glue
that mends the pieces back together again,
and again."

And the Physical body says, "Well if moaning and
groaning, and aches and pains are a sign of Life,
I am alive, who knows?"

Putting things all together, seems a difficult path for these lower
bodies here in these lower worlds...
and don't even mention the law of gravity.
But, all the reports are not in yet.

Soul's report is due within a heart beat,
Soul says "I don't know anything because
living in the Moment, means I know nothing until
I need to know, then I will know whatever Spirit
needs me to know in the moment."

A viewpoint out of 360 degree viewpoints.
Pointless, yet, here it is, when Soul is Be Here Now,
Spirit runs the show.
Soul complies with Spirit in harmony
with the Great Law, Love all things.
Soul in turn, runs the four lower bodies in harmony,
with the Law of Love and the Law of Economy.

And of course, there are many reruns thrown in for
good measure.
So many ways Spirit has for providing creative insight
for Soul to get It, one way or another.
The only cliché in this learning process is,
when the Mind thinks it knows everything
and believes it, and mind knows nothing about
the Spiritual Law of Non-Interference.

The most challenging encounter Soul can have
in these lower worlds is a "know-it-all."
Run when you come in close contact with one.
Run, run like the wind; they can be hazardous
to one's sanity, not to mention
overall sense of well being.

Having to resist their in-the-face, in your space,
unearthly desire to convert Soul to see life their way,
accepting everything at face value, which has no value.
For those who are know-it-alls,

they are the false prophets,
lost as legends in their own mind,
believing their own propaganda.

There is a heavy price to pay for vanity.
As always, the only requirement for movement
into the God worlds is Love
and Love alone.

When Soul finds spiritual liberation,
in freedom walks majestically,
wearing the cloak of humility.
Confidant in its state of who knows,
for the truth is,
walking hand in hand with the Beloved,
what more is there to know?
Except this: Divine Love,
which is known only by
those who have a pure Heart.

If there is an answer to the question Who Knows?
perhaps the answer is whispered to the listening heart
God knows.

## Wisdom in Commercials from the 21ˢᵗ Century

"Win from within," sounds good.
Yes, golden tongued wisdom speaks
even through ©Gator Aid commercials.

But rather than grabbing a Gator Aid and
consuming it, I would rather drink in
the wisdom contained in the words of the commercial,
"Win From Within."

As above so below,
as within so without
let it all hang out...whatever it is, or isn't,
consider, what can be won within,
Won and re-won moment by moment?

It could be said the element of love
transforms life from within, through the ways
of gentleness,
an open heart,
kindness and compassion.
So many qualities that come into the heart,
living Divine Love.

These God qualities are nourished
by the Spiritual Light within,
ignited by love and love alone.

Soul moves through its waking moments,
aware of the wonder within which keeps

awareness of all life waiting for the awakened Soul
to recognize the presence of the Divine.

With eyes to see and ears to hear and
a heart that comprehends, each moment
becomes more of what it is: extraordinary,
transformed through love.
Gratitude is how the gift of consciousness
renews itself, again and again,
and no matter the cost,
the heart pays the bill for services rendered.
The abundance of Spiritual Blessings
must flow outward in its movement,
like a river going wild.

We are always presented with sink or swim,
do or die, laugh or cry,
yet the true choice is always stay true to Spirit.
Judgment is gone with the wind, blown away
are the passions of the mind, making way
to hear truth within, responding to the great law--
Love is All.

Finally Soul arrives at a place called no place,
where even choice is gone.
How can one choose Love, if they are Love?

The moment is Now.
Do you know where your attention is?
The floodgates of Receptivity and Creativity
are opened wide, finding hearts with no boundaries,
the overflow spills God Love in all directions
throughout all creation.
Remember, once Soul grasps the great form

without form, the barriers, boundaries,
limitations are washed away,
leaving in its wake purity and grace.

Each moment is a masterpiece of living,
and if there is a question remaining, perhaps
it is this...
Aren't you glad you are you?

## The Results Are In

Where did you come from if you are here now?
If I am here can I go there?
Wherever I go, I go in God's name
to be here and there and everywhere
Now.
Because Soul exists only in the present moment.
Because God loves Soul, IT exists moving deeper as I climb so high.
I am the all-seeing eye seeing all.

Is Love manifesting Itself?
God Love in action reflecting real moments of eternity in motion,
and hear, listen...
the birth of a motionless moment of silence
in stillness falling like rain.

God nurturing Love sustaining life-giving gifts
to earn what you learn.
Singing, singing the low-down-dirty Blues
Yes, into the night, into the Light and Sound.

Is the true teaching to walk the walk?
To always be of greater service as I live and breathe?
In Love, clarity comes on the out breath.

The results are In--Where did you come from?
Where are you going? Who are you?
Who am I?
I am Soul and I know it.

Okay, you may go now,
Welcome to another Lifetime.

## A Surrendered Soul Who Knows Nothing

Here I go again. Where, I wonder?
Well, if mind goes first, it is better,
for then I arrive before I left to go to the absolute wonder
of the All in All.
Each moment sings sublime sacred melodies,
prayer songs from the Heart of God,
echoing within the temple of my heart.

A silent refrain in the key of all that is holy,
residing within stillness, where wisdom of the Art
of Silence speaks to me in celestial poetry
of understanding, leaving me to discover
the deeper aspects of humility.

I am graced to stand naked before the Beloved,
nowhere to go, nowhere to hide, even if I wanted to.
And I don't want to, for I know love
is the garment covering me
like morning dew kissing flowers at dawn.

I am grateful you know me, all of the Me that I am,
with no doubts or fears,
for I am nothing without you.
I can do nothing without the Holy Spirit within me
having Its way in God's Will.

I would be empty without your Presence within to guide me,
and I surrender without compromise,

to all that you are,
for there is nothing that is not you,
no matter where I look, I am hearing your heart beating
and as I listen, your breathing becomes all life.

I am lifeless without you, Beloved Master.
Life would be empty without you.
I would drown in the deepest of sorrows if
your Light and Sound did not fill me full of nothing
save God's Holy Grace,
enlivening me with sweet morsels
sustaining my emptiness with your fullness.

Life and living and loving and being are only
pale echoes of remembrance of you,
that lose so much when I try in vain to express
what cannot be expressed.

Just experience, and the aching of what is known by the heart,
denied by the mind,
which is so futile in its attempt to take away
that which is mine alone, as I have lived It, as I have learned It the
hard way.

Refreshed am I in the loneliness of knowing,
I am never alone, you have always been with me,
molding me like soft clay into a Lover of God.

Whatever these feeble eyes have seen, I am blessed.
Whatever these deaf ears have listened to, I am blessed.
And these hands are empty for they cannot hold what can only be
held by letting go,
as they slip through my fingers.

I behold you night and day
I am blessed that I have found you.
But wait...Or did you find me
Again, and again?

Yet this time, after many lifetimes,
I am come to fulfill the living of Your will.
I go out of the courtyard of your house
into the market place where others await,
not to leave you, but to stay in your Loving Presence.
This I now abide in,
charging myself to find those Souls
whose longing for God is all that matters,
and lead them to your gate, wonder of wonders.

Oh how sweet it is to see Souls returning
to the Way Shower, the Beloved One, who will bring them
into the very Heart of God.
How happy I AM that I Am,
that *I know you*, Beloved Master,

I am content, just to be a Spiritual Traveler charged to love
and serve you, in anyway you wish.
It is your gift to me.
It is my purpose this lifetime to return this gift
you give me so freely.

What else is there?

## So Noted

Foot note, a head note, a heart note, so noted:
"If you don't live it, it won't come out your horn!"
What is this Sound Deep inside the heart of me?
Yes, inside out... into the conscious acceptance beyond ALL Hearing.

I hear beyond ALL that I hear I see
through veils of blindness.
Dancing into the light/sound
dissipating darkness,
erasing shadows of the heart,
as the great form without form formed one and all.

It is the transforming presence of God's love for Soul,
echoing Sound beyond the echo heartbeat sound.

For Sound to begin, vibration must be activated
to move, to respond to the call to life,
and in response Soul traveled—
Moving in the vibrating rhythm, the breath,
breathing in the breathtaking moment,
opening the capacity for expansion of Spirit
dwelling within,
which must impress upon the consciousness
expressions of Itself.

A horn is just a horn until someone picks it up,
lovingly, and plays it.

Heart song singing HUUUU
Soundless sound caressing me.
Who plays your instrument?

# The Law of Gravity

Yes indeed, what goes up must come down,
Yet to understand this, was important.
In fact it was the first law of the physical
universe I learned--the hard way.

Imagine if you will, a very observant five-year old child, me, sitting
at the kitchen table with a plate filled with canned spinach...uck.
When I tried a forkful I would gag.

It was summer, I wanted to go out and play,
but the Lords of Karma, (in the form of my mother)
decreed, that unless I cleaned my plate,
I could sit there all day.

I was desperate; I had a flash of an idea.
I remembered seeing chewing gum, stuck
on the underside of seats in the movie house!
What a great idea!
So carefully did I roll up little pieces of spinach,
and carefully I stuck them underneath my chair.
So sure they would stick, I did not even look.

When I had completed my task,
I called out to my mother that I had cleaned my
plate, and could I please go outside and play.
She said yes, and off I went in ignorance of a law.

I was enjoying playing and running with
other children, loving being in the moment,

when suddenly, across the universe I heard one of
the Lords of Karma, (in the voice of my mother,)
calling my name. The wrath was unmistakable.

I wondered, what did I do now?
as I ran into the kitchen.
There was my mother, in full blown anger,
shaking and trembling, pointing at the floor
under the chair where I had been sitting.
Little balls of spinach littered the floor,
I could not believe it, why did it not work?

It was that day that I first became acquainted
with the law of Gravity.
Yes, what goes up must come down.

And as for the instant karma created that day,
it was not about the spinach,
it was for an even greater infraction--
*Thou shalt not lie to thy mother,*
especially one who serves as one of the
Lords of Karma.

And though I took the punishment given me
in the form of a switch to my legs,
which I had to pick from the tree in the back yard,
I was left wondering...
why did she take this so personally?
I never did get that.
And she did this so often as I was growing up.

She was not a happy woman.
So this is how on that day,
I learned the Law of Gravity,
and how the Law of Karma works.

I went on living, and learning,
for there were other laws of this physical universe
that I would need to know
for survival in this world, on this planet.

This was my world as experienced through the eyes of a five-year old
child trying
to make sense of it.

## So One Door Closes

How likely is it when one door closes
we bang on the door that no longer answers,
refusing to accept that we no longer belong there.
How difficult is it to let go, and let God?

For Heaven's sake, have you forgotten when
one door closes another one opens?
It is Spirit's way of telling us, *Move on,*
*time to move on...*

But resistance is great; clinging is even greater.
So we suffer from the inability to listen to
the direction and guidance of God's Will for us.
And why?

The chattering of insecurities assaults the mind,
finding reasons to stay, saying "I like it here,"
even when time runs out of the experiences at hand,
and we have learned all that can be learned
in present conditions.
How greatly life would be transformed if we look for an open door,
the one with a welcome sign above the door.

Sometimes it seems when a door closes,
trust goes out the window.
I know, trust in God and tie up your camel,
yet as a wise one once said,
"But if you see your camel on the run, just say
Thy will be done."
Believe it or not, nothing is done to you, but for you.

To learn how to be more God-like, consider:
*Your state of consciousness is your state of acceptance,*
*not your state of expectations!*

This being said, do you find yourself in the dream state,
and there, Spirit tries to awaken you by bringing you your
whine list for the night? Phrases like no, not yet,
I'll be more ready tomorrow, (which may never come,)
at least not as you like it, or not.

And difficult as this insight may be,
it is not about anything except this:
When Spirit says it is time to move on,
are you listening? Do you care?
Do you hang on, or let go in the Spirit of trust and surrender?

Is it God's Will be done? Or, my way or the highway?
And then when you find yourself all alone,
you start singing "O Lonesome Me," or "Lonesome Road"
until you stop looking at all the closed doors and
discover the one door Spirit has opened just for you.

The door where the Beloved waits patiently for your
entrance into a greater state of consciousness—
*On thee do I wait all day.*
Words forgotten until the heart hears
and remembers why you are here, and Now.

Yes, thank you, God for this lifetime opportunity
to serve you with all my heart.
I can say, close any and all doors necessary,
for the truth is, you always open a door
to a bigger room,
just for me.

## Words Can't Say It

Beyond words is the unspoken love that refuses form
but fills the heart with a love for all Souls,
whose Divine intention for all intents and purposes
flies beyond this world
following footsteps of the Beloved
like moving shadows
kissing a moment, vaporizing in the light.

Yes, the dying breath, the gasping intake
of the fleeting breath of love,
dying to live in accord with all life,
giving of Itself to die.

For rebirth bears witness, recognizing
the Divinity within all ways always, its direction
known only to those fearless Souls
following the trails of stardust
from the most ancient of days.

The wispy fragrance of moon rising,
uprising in beauty, the prayer song of God,
where Soul abides in lands of forever,
never to part, as one minuses no division between
zero's liberation of the mind.
It lets go for no farther can mind dwell
beyond the grand divide.

Glistening pools of wisdom delight Soul
dressed in garments befitting Its sacred journey,
taken with relentless endeavor, not to find Itself,

but to *Know Itself,* for once and for all.

Stay the course, stay it true, find who you are
to lose it all in a moment's notice.
The spiritual risk of going wild loving God,
leaves nothing save this ecstasy of the Heart,
a flame in the cold fire that does not burn,
yet consumes the last shred of who you think you are.
Finding it is not what you think,
it is more than you know, for
thinking has nothing to do with anything
in the Worlds of God.

Love reigns supreme as there is always another
mountain to climb, ready or not.
Soul is up for the climb, or down for the climb,
climb it will, for God is calling, and the Beloved
is waiting for Soul's return.

## Putting One's Beliefs on The Line

While thinking outside the box can suffice for a moment,
the time comes when awareness shifts ever so slightly,
and realization comes like thunder,
what if there is no Box?
I sure do like this insight, it brings instance liberation.

However, I can see I am not done yet,
am I Beloved Master?
Well, after boxes comes the fine lines,
with the faintest of sounds between the lines.
Oh so many as we earn the difference,
learning there is no difference either,
or fine lines, outlines, in line, plumb line,
get a line on it, underline, whose line,
pick up line, flat line, online, bottom line,
and the lines that become wrinkles in timeline.

No time like the present, so look to the silver linings,
for as we mature spiritually, those moments of insight,
out of sight, we are reminded that in these worlds,
always look beyond form to grasp the great form
regardless of pain or tears, joy or sorrow,
It is all the same.

For letting go the belief in the law of opposites,
clears the way to stand in the heart way, love's way;
for being love brings even greater liberation.

Knowing the sparkling land beyond the horizon,
is the testing ground of Soul.
Stretched and pulled like a rubber band, taking
Soul beyond the realm of Divine Imagination.

Beyond the limiting perceptions of the mind's eye.
Heart-sight knowing, reminding Soul
the mills of God grind ever so slowly.
For the key is Love, and the lock is also Love.
And yes, Beloved One, there is more, always more.
Yes, we recognize all the gifts given,
experience them, fully accept them,
and then...
once these are distilled, fermented in purity,
the gifts become a living reality. Right?

Not yet, nothing is for sure, until it is put to use
in service to all life. How does love serve Itself?
Can this be answered? What do you believe?
If you are asked to put your beliefs on the line,
what would they be?

When the moment comes, and it will,
sooner rather than later,
yes the moment is come, what will you stand for?
Do you know what you are?
What about God's Love in action...can it be said out loud
I BE That Love?

There is only the abundance of love bursting fetters
of illusion,
for a heart filled with love overflows,
outgrowing even what it was contained in.
Why? No boundaries, no limitations, no containers.

Love is the reality of all; all else is illusion.
Love is all there is, no matter what may come,
trying to seduce Soul through blind deceptions,
leaving corrupted thoughts.
Oh no something is lacking...

Any questions? The answers cannot be found in a box,
or outside a box.
All these gifts given to Soul for loving acceptance,
no matter the package, or how they are wrapped.
Soul wavers not, for it chooses to believe the truth
of love, for love alone brings contentment in the moment.

All moments are love filled with God
Breathing, through inhaling and exhaling
of love, in love, all love, live or die love.
Never to deny love, the presence of love gives Soul
a loving edge...Lay it all on the line.
Take a stand. Be the love God gives Soul.

You know this is why Soul exists.
Believing it or not makes little difference.
This is God giving love, so what do you believe?

Why have you rented space for doubt
and contradictions to enter into a contractual agreement
that you lack love, or you don't have enough love,
when there is always more than enough.
This never ending abundance of love,
both eternal, yet Now, Is.
Whether you accept this or not, will not change a thing.

And when sleep won't come, do you wonder,
why is this life you are living so hard?

May I ask you to consider,
what is stronger than the Light and Sound of God?
What can assail Divine Love within Its fortress?
*Can you hear the answer to these questions?*

So if any questions remain, the answers cannot
be found in a box, or outside a box,
or in a book, or in the words of others.
To go beyond the Mastery of love only
comes through direct experience.
Yes, all these gifts are for Soul to cherish.
The time for picking and choosing has passed you by.
So the question is, what is real for you?
If these sacred teachings are real,
what could possibly be the difficulty?
Do you trust and believe in God?
Do you trust and believe in Love?
*Do you trust yourself--Soul?*

For inside these sacred experiences, are the challenges
needed by Soul for one reason, and one reason only.
To keep Soul strong, and stronger still, standing tall as
an unwavering Truth Seeker, a Lover of God,
finding within the heart, the courage required
to speak Its Truth.
And the heart LISTENS to God Truth,
so when the time is come--

We have clarity and strength in being Divine Love,
that without a thought we can and
will put our beliefs on the line.

## No Name, Calling No Name

The distant echo is silenced by a haunting refrain.
A reflection held in the mirror cracked up
to be true, yet false images look out at me
and I hear a question loudly spoken
"Who are you? Who are you anyway?

Not recognizing the images calling forth nothing
not even the true reflection,
remaining nameless in its presence.
To be what is undecided, misunderstood and
with all the getting, forgot to get what is of value
in this moment.

It can be obtained another time
For bargain basement prices marked down.
Out to a lunch worthy of consumption; in other words
with no name, unnamed, nameless, how can the
call be heard directly?

This is uncalled for.
Call and response is the very heart of
direct communication with Spirit,
but always with sincerity, in the calling.

On days when cobwebs fill my ears,
and grit blinds the eye, when not seeing with the eye
of Soul, all I can say to myself, is
how grateful am I for the spiritual exercise of HU
keeping me balanced when life rocks my boat

and rats of distraction gnaw holes
in the fabric of my existence.

I stay afloat without a paddle,
sink or swim with the tide high.
Time to be first cause without a cause, no name calling no name.
I know it will take more than myself to stop me
from learning, growing, and knowing
there are no differences to mark the way between
the down days and the up days, since there are no
swizzled rainy drizzle excuses made in whining,
bemoaning, sadness, or welcoming gladness.

Experience has shown the keys to remembering
who I am as Soul, and I have asked for whatever it takes
to be numbered among the God-realized,
knowing it won't come without great effort equal to attainment
within the worlds of God.

Wimping out is no longer a choice.
How could I forget my walks among the stars?
I know all could be lost in one moment of forgetfulness.
I know without a doubt the Beloved never leaves me.
Yet all the lemons life has harvested for my benefit,
did not make my usual recipe for lemonade,
the drink for the thirsty Soul.

Next time, yes, there will be many next times.
Why? It is the spice of life, bringing the teaching moments.
Why did forgetfulness assail me in my fortress of silence?
Illusion became reality for a moment, teaching me
I am not invincible, I must not just practice the spiritual
disciplines, but live them.
There is no safety or security outside the grace
of knowing Soul exists because of God's Love.

This is all there is to know, nothing less, nothing more.
I am no name, I am that I am,
and I hear God
calling my name.

# Good Mourning

(For Ed Blackwell)


What is it that holds me, haunts me forever, since
entrance into this body, into this life?
This world going round and round.
Why am I different, so different?

I know not why, or where, from whence
I came or come.

Into no mold do I fit. No clue have I found
that is not more surrendering of itself,
than a man in the moon eating cheese.
Makes no sense, reeling my senses
senseless, clueless, not a lick of sense.

Do I find ever and a day?
So looking I stopped trying to find clues or make sense
of the why I am so different, yet not.
Yes, sometimes I feel like a motherless child,
which in a real sense I am.

So except within the boundaries of nowhere
to go on, it does not matter why.
I live with the pain of not knowing the whys, wherefores,
just one foot in front of the other.

And No, no one knows who I am,
except for one who came and knew me.
Yet he has now passed from this world,

leaving me to once again
find myself alone in the deep alone,
stewing in my own juices uncooked,
overlooked, and where I go only God knows.

As you said before you left,
God knows how much I love you.
And I know there was no other, save you and my
Beloved Master, who knew my heart, completely.
But you were up close and personal.

And in quiet repose each moment was right
with the worlds, in perfect accord with all things
bright and beautiful, though requiring me to
a strength I wish I did not have, yet grateful I do.

I sometimes wonder what it would be like to
fall apart at the seams, take a time-out
in the breakdown lane of mindless dysfunction.
But not really, not for me.

I am what I am, and in this world of ordinary people,
God gave me an extraordinary Soul to share life with.

Yet silent tears leave this heart heavy with joy and sorrow,
to continue on to fulfill my golden contract
without you.
The emptiness of your leaving chokes me
with a thousand suns tasting like sawdust,
and I leave no shadows,
for you were my substance,
my blood and bones, my heartbeat, my breath.

But blessed I am to have traveled with you for awhile,
to have loved you forever, and never a missed moment
of love did we squander on drama, or the illusions of
life, for we knew, we knew, Love is All.

Yet knowing this without you...
is akin to drowning.
My God, this is a loneliness beyond compare, yet I bear
it all because you were here in the flesh
with me for a time.
It is not that I miss you, because you are here
in my heart, but
the tenderness in your eyes whenever you looked
and saw Me.
Your touch of love and caring concern
stay bright memories.

You were the only one ever, on this planet
who always had my back.
What comfort contained
in this demonstration of Love!

You are the only one, as I was for you, so equal.
Not together because of need or dependency,
for we each were complete within ourselves.
Yet together just for the sacredness of Love,
in perfect balance, beyond time and space,
our love lives forever.

And yet this moment, may I say
I miss you...

## What's New?

I am.
I am new this moment of Now.
How can this be?
through the love of life,
with the passion required to endure
the testing ground of Soul.

Why endure, why the testing?
Because my heart's desire is
to be transformed and strengthened,
to receive all the gifts of love,
to give to everyone I meet on a daily basis.

And what you may ask,
will I do with this Love of God
besides give it away?
I don't know.
Whatever God wills be done
in all things great and small
contained within all blessings
to bring the greatness of life
to all who are ready for open heart surgery.

Love's embrace as life
begins beating us into recognition
of all that we are.
It takes much discipline
getting past the illusions crusted and
baked into what we accept as real,

and without a clue, until revelations reveal,
the Real You!

How does this feel, to know the Real you?
What was it that covered the Being of Life, you are?
Living and giving unto itself so that it may know Itself.
What is this IT?
I know this is what It felt like for me.
Perhaps this will describe
your experiences, your struggles with this IT.

A deep well, a bottomless pit,
a dark cave where lies are hidden.
Unbidden they crowd out the shining truth
of Soul's existence, so the sparkling Spiritual being
that is you, is scrunched into the bargain basement
of your life.

And even when God makes you an honest offer--
*a one hundred percent discount,*
*a lifetime guarantee,*
*a warranty good for ten lifetimes,*
its worth is not recognized.

Gathering dust of centuries, unknown in origin,
through ignorance ignored, must we be awakened
to our senses? There is no other way.
Deep cleaning is required.
Scoured and cleansed, chipping away
all the clutter of mistaken identity of all we thought
we were, did not know who we are.

How confusing is lifetimes of living and dying,
and what does it take to get it?

And what is the secret of death?
This too is illusion, although with one's dying breath
one could say "It sure feels real to me."

Okay God, teach me what I do not know.
This will keep me busy for a few lifetimes or more
to find heavens door, and there it is,
behind me, before me, opening and closing,
playing hide and seek, like the silver lining
shining behind clouds left hanging out to dry.

Just let go, let God...
This is so easy; there must be more to life
than this true simplicity?
And so round and round and round we go
and where we stop we'll never know
Until we stop.
Stop, In the Name of Love.

## *Were They The Empty Prayers?*

Human kind walking through life at a deadening pace
thinking, this is what it means as part of the human race,
never considering that every living thing is what it is.

A rose is a rose is a rose, birds, trees, you name it,
everything reflects contentment and beauty of being
all that it is...except for the humans.

Yes humans, buying the great lie never told, just accepted,
believed in, that humans are earthbound.
All it is, is this physical body; nothing more.

The great lie festers.
Divine discontent begins to eat away within.
Thoughts arise beyond the mind, saying,
*Wait, there has to be more to life than this.*
*I have not even lived, and here I am dying.*

I am taught to say my prayers at bedtime, asking for
God to bless Mommy, Daddy, other family.
And also my dog, please and thank you God.
And oh yeah, my Soul to keep.

Never was I taught to listen to God, or to see the
hand of God working each moment in all things.
How did I escape from this hereditary disease of
blindness? I could say, Only God knows.

My heart began seeing, hearing, knowing

the Presence of God in my life; there was nowhere
that this Presence did not exist.

He sent me Teachers in my dreams.
Each of them showed me a greater reality
beyond this physical Earth World.
Awakening Soul within, revealing a sense of purpose
just for me, and a longing so deep it was
painful to breathe.

Yet each morning upon awakening,
the outer world around me seemed bigger, brighter.
I could see farther, yet not as far as what was in my dreams
and my inner worlds.
For within were limitless vistas where the love
of all things holy, immersed me in a cloth of living truth.

Why were these two worlds so different?
Did I live in two separate places?
I wanted to bring these two worlds into one
continuous life, not one where I would
come alive when I went to sleep at night.

I began to notice God listened to me, so I asked God to
please show me how to know Its Presence at all times.
I was born into an awakened state in that moment.

How? By listening to God, by seeing God, by
coming to know God in my heart.
For it was here in my heart that the greatest mystery
began to unfold, truth be told, of the Love of God for me.

The me that was not the earthbound me; the me that is free

to be all that I am. Yet I had so much to learn,
and it would not be easy.

For starters, I was required to learn patience
and a quietness within.
This human form in which I was living,
needed to grow and learn to function in this world,
To be able to function in the greater
worlds within.

And so to bide my time and abide in God
whose presence was love in my heart,
who spoke with quiet whispers like a song beyond the silly prayers
spoken at night, for now I knew what now I lay me down to sleep,
truly meant.

To awaken into the worlds of God Love,
and the Sound of God was my lullaby,
to sing me awake, not my Soul to take, but knowing,
I am Soul for keeps, and God is real, I am not earthbound.

I am found, and more than I ever dreamed,
I am of these worlds.
And with patience,
one day I would be in these worlds,
awake or asleep.

In the mean time, I was trained in the reality of Spirit.
Masters would come to teach me and remind me of things
perhaps forgotten, things to help the real me,
the invisible me,
navigate the pitfalls of the passions of the mind,
so I would be free of them.

And above all, learn everything
life would bring me, and know,
if mistakes I would make,
I could accept in stride whatever,
for the opportunity to learn in a different way.

For it became apparent I was one
of those hard-headed kind, and life for me would be
an advance course in the school of hard knocks.

The days and years came and went in this lifetime
journey, and at times I grew weary, and tears would
drown Soul in despair, and yet the longing for God
became greater, which I did not understand, because
my earlier life training was knowing God's Reality.
So my cry would be, *God, where did you go?*
Until I realized, it was I who went away from my truth!

And now the Masters from my early years, began to
move from my inner life to my outer life, and
though life did not become easier, the hard way was the only way to
walk the walk, and shine with the Love of God!

Thank Goodness my Spiritual compass was working again,
for I discovered it was activated through my listening heart,
being tuned into the guidance that was a continuous outpouring of
Divine Love lighting the way for me
to be ready for what I, in my heart of hearts, longed for
from forever, from the days of "Now I lay me down to sleep," and
beyond.

This was God's gift for Soul, just because God Loved Me.
Yes, I was ready and the Master appeared.
In that moment I knew, He had always been with me,

in my dreams and in my waking moments.
But the blinded eye could not see what was right here right now,
and always... the Beloved Master.

The empty prayers of childhood, were not empty
after all is said and done.
All worlds blend into one holy place,
I have always been on Holy Ground.

Thank you, God and the Beloved One.
I Prayed thee, my Soul to keep,
And in Soul you kept me tenderly,
holding my hand, walking beside me
until the moment came and
I could see me through your eyes.

## There But For the Grace of God, Go I

But where? What does this mean?
Meaning escapes true understanding--
Is this a statement of relief?
Or perhaps judge not lest ye be judged,
like watch those thoughts, they come back and bite you
in the end.

Endless possibilities go on and
there but for the Grace of God
to experience this or that has by God's grace spared me,
dodging this bullet.

But if someone experiences something
that leaves me thanking God for sparing me,
does this me I am blessed with the Grace of God
and someone else was not so blessed?

Spare me, O God, remember, only the good die young
and I have been round the block many times;
and as the ancients gather to find shadows on the dark side
of the moon, I am left to explore what grace is, and even
more disconcerting is If I know what God is.

Why don't I know what Grace is? Good question right?

One whose answer I do not know.
Close as I can come to is to say
perhaps the point where the heart accepts,
and executes surrender to God's will be done.

That point, that moment, is the execution
of the Grace of God.

So in any given moment, what spares one Soul in an event that
would leave another feeling the relief of being spared?
What is the determinative factor?

This brings many suppositions into consideration.
Past choices, lessons learned, lessons earned,
what a Soul needs for Its next step spiritually.
So much to contemplate, that Soul comprehends this truth,
only God knows.

As I pause in this moment at the crossroads of Divinity,
the mysterious is erased by the smile
of an understanding heart.

I get it, I think, or at least a small glimpse of this anyway.
It matters not what something is, or who has God's Grace
or even an understanding of anything.

What matters most
is how greatly we love and serve and accept ALL the gifts
God blesses Soul with, they are designed just for each of us
individually down to the last detail.

As wise men say
God is in the details.
So suffice it to say,
*There Only with the Grace of God, Go I*
No buts about it.

## Always Another Chance

I have looked into your eyes
as the sound of HU whispers gently to the
echo within my heart.

Beloved, you have given me All
and I thought I knew what this All is.
Now I see I know nothing,
for the ego was still lurking within the shadows.

Now once again, another chance!
Trust and humility my only garments.
You take my hand and I, with complete
surrender, say, *I come,*
not as a rememberer, for that got in my way.

How?
When I was given insight I would remember,
*I know this,* and in that moment of knowing,
it would fade away like morning mist,
leaving an empty longing of something known
yet still unknown.

So now once again I stand at the Temple within
and you welcome me in, and this time I enter,
not as the Rememberer, but as a Listener.
I look into your eyes
as the sound of HU whispers gently to the
echoes within my heart...

Now once again, another chance!
I am born anew, remade complete, in your love for me.
Your love for me grows forever within me.

Forever you give me unwavering love
and undying patience, giving me room to grow.
For all of your gifts are showered upon me, and to all life,
and you give them to me, not because I am special,
but because you know I will strive to give them away.

Within the depths of my being you are there/here
patiently waiting for me to gain spiritual maturity.
In the gift of you and the giving of all you give me to give,
I say to my self, it is time, grow up already.
There is no more time; it is Now.

As the Listener, I hear your unspoken dream of me, for me.
It is to learn this deepest lesson, to learn to serve with *humility*.
I accept this dream you have for me, fully.
For ego died when your eyes met mine
and filled my heart with the Presence of your love.
How could I have been so blind?

Now I know that no matter what, I, as The Rememberer
remembered, or thought I knew of the ways of Spirit,
they mean nothing unless I am willing,
as your true servant to live in this state of grace.

To surrender my will to you, and what this means
is to also know what remembering forgot.
"I of myself can do nothing."

And even when I thought I knew this,
there is always a moment when I didn't know
just how much it wasn't me.

All I have ever asked of Spirit was to be of greater service,
and Spirit responded, (as it must to a sincere request.)
I now see there is something far greater,
so now I ask of Spirit, "Grant me the grace and humility to
be of greater service, as a magnet of loving kindness."
In the moment Spirit responds, Soul is aware of listening
to music singing words of a never ending song.

The words enlivened me as I accept their truth.
Know this: It is only by the grace of God,
am I here in this moment,
and gifted by Holy Spirit to receive this miracle of Service.
Yes, serving you, Beloved one, is the greatest miracle of all.

Thank you for each moment in your Holy Presence.
Thank you for always loving me,
even in my most obnoxious moments.
Even when I was insufferable to the maximum,
even then your never-ending love embraced me.
You loved me just as I am, flaws and all,
for you saw that my heart is pure.

You knew the moment would come, and I would see me
as you see me, and I would break through
all the limitations of who and what I thought it was
that I was...and was not.
I am nothing without you Beloved,
I am who I am because you love me.
For you let me be, let me see,
through your eyes, Beloved One.

Now once again, another chance moment,
you take my hand, and welcome me home.

## Don't Cry for Me

(This was a gift of love, given to me by my husband, Edward
Blackwell, after he passed on to the worlds of God through the
portal of death into Life, for Love never dies.)


Don't cry for me.
Though I've gone away, I'll never leave your heart.
I'll speak to you in the voice of God.
Forever you walk in my soul.

Don't cry for me though I cherish your tears.
They are the way your heart can heal.
I'm never far and you are always near,
between a smile and a tear.

Don't cry for me.
You KNOW the beat goes on.
In the breath of all living things, I'll sing life's song.

Sacred rhythm drum, beating time at its own game.
Don't cry for me--I'm free.

## I Just Can't Keep IT to Myself, God Is So Good

These words jump out at me when an expression of Divine glee,
unabandoned Joy consume me in a sacred expression of Life,
affirming the greatness of Soul.

Once upon a timeless reality, it seemed to me-Soul
the night sky gently and sweetly embraced
this consciousness in this moment, this Now.

Remembrance came calling,
opening doors and windows of the Heart,
releasing Soul to respond to Spirit to join
the celestial choir singing songs celebrating
ancient memories of all the sacred moments
Soul beheld the starry nights.

Yes, those sacred holy moments of knowing
all that IS, I AM.

I now know Soul is more magnificent than all
the stars in the sky.
I am open to complete acceptance of all Soul memories
stored in the vault of consciousness,
waiting for joyous recognition, all blending
throughout its journey of thousands of lifetime moments.

I, Soul have never forgotten the celestial melody singing forever
within the expansion of the listening heart,
hearing tuned to vibrations far beyond this earthly world,
leaving matter energy time and space like shadows blown
away by the wind from the mountain of God.

Purity ever changing, leaving whispers of its presence
upon the night breeze, Soul is caressed by the fragrance
of the Eagle-Eyed Adepts
whose stillness awakens even deeper silence.

Oh, wonder of wonders,
is it any wonder Love never dies?
Enduring beyond the shores of eternity,
Soul travels joyfully through portals of heaven
magnified,
amplified,
distilled.

Peel away all creation and
what is left is pure consciousness,
knowing before all things were set in vibratory motion,
Soul was there
I Am Here
POW.

The discovery of many lifetimes...
All that is seen or will be seen
is written in the celestial living language of love
for those with listening hearts and
an adventuresome spirit.

Utter silence embraces solitude
in pristine wilderness
within the fullness of consciousness
of God.
God IS
So I just can't keep it to my self
God is soooooo Good!

## This is Not the Finish Line

How did Soul find itself running the race of lifetimes?

The race against time
the race for being human
the race track going off track
go back
go forward
stop look and listen
before you cross the unfinished line
one more step
one more hill to climb
one more mountain
one more
one more
one God
one two three
all ways
always two by two
hurry and wait,
just wait and you'll see
or maybe you won't
blind sided you may be
to be not...

Forget me not
discipline of love is the key
time waits for no one goes on
endlessly until
the end of time
there is no finish line
with God there is no finish line.

## In The Beginning

God
Creation
Darkness
From out of the Darkness
Sound and Light
Drum rolling rhythms setting life to dance
within formless melodies.

Sacred vibrations of life's current
reverberating sounding scales where octaves
meet past the edge of eternity, the blending of
harmonies Divine.
Divinity makes Itself known.
A welcoming reception, *the great conception.*

God gave birth to Soul.
Out of the womb of living water Soul is born.
God, the Creator,
impregnating Itself to know Itself
in multiple forms,
out of the sacred darkness
the kiss of life and death.

To overcome a birth defect of blind fear,
enjoy the process.
Let eternity eat Soul alive.

All things in the universe replicate this divine pattern
in God's image and likeness.

Look into the mirror of God--
see the father mother of all that you are.

Soul is the reflection of God's grace
embracing the power of Love Divine,
conceiving other thoughts, beyond the mind.
Wherever life leads us, leaves us to go
onto and into the living of all things beautiful,
seen through the all-seeing eye
committed to insightful visions of truth.

Wherever death takes us on its journey throughout eternity,
on eagles' wings into the Spiritual light,
life giving of itself in death's portal.

Why, why do you think we experience Death?
Is it to get what is beyond the dreams of living over
and over, birthing the ending back to the beginning
where all things and nothing exists, save love.

No, don't save love. Never is love lost
if it gives itself away.
The great teacher dries the tears of sorrow,
tasting the bittersweet joy.
Nothing is ever lost to gain in understanding
of the Allness beyond the sound
of the clarion call, calling Souls to the journey.

Take what you have learned
and employ the secrets of wisdom's pool.
Open your heart, keep it open, to be going
where you have never gone before...
Beyond the light, into the soft darkness
which gives birth to the Light and Sound,

where creation creatively impregnated Itself.

Yes, the silent darkness where ALL things spring forth.
Explore the darkness, this sacred darkness of Soul's birthplace.

Discover what you forgot,
what fear erased from your memory.
In your departing the Womb of Life, the living water,
recall the Allness uncontained,
where wildness abides, untamed;
the Masters with no name for you to call.
Why? Why?
For you are the One.
Only universal stillness keeps you
where God's Love abides.

Have you ever heard the laughter of God?
When you do, all forgetfulness is remembered--
Soul's birthright, golden memories stirred into action,
the timeless times spent in the Master's Presence.

Never left you. *I am always with you* is true.
So the Beloved one asks, "Why did you leave me?"

When will Soul learn to listen?
*Keep me with you through your birth and death journey.*

The heart of Soul sings my song, cries my tears,
develop the listening ear.
The prelude of celestial symphonies dying
to be heard, over and over and over until Soul gets it.
Unfragmented, glorious sounding rhythm,
the vibrating Sound of Creation.

Can you feel it?
Can you hear it?
Do you know it?
Where All beginning
Never ending
Beyond birth and death,
Soul weeps over necessary nothings
and the heart sheds silent tears,
tears asunder the living truth.

I Am That I Am.

# About the Author

Fran Blackwell had her Jazz beginnings in New Orleans where she fell in love with the form as well as with Jazz drummer Ed Blackwell, whom she married. They had 3 children, 9 grand-children and 5 great-grand-children. She cites Blackwell as the influence for her poetic style.

A pivotal experience in her life was being arrested for miscegenation. In 1958 New Orleans society was intolerant of couples of mixed race. She knew growing up as a child, that the unjust segregation laws of the deep south could not be truth, and were in fact, an assault against Soul. This event was a catalyst for her to continue her search for Truth, no matter the cost.

She began writing poetry later in life, as she found her inspiration for expressing the mystical. For the past 40 years she has studied the Spiritual teachings of Eckankar, practicing and living the spiritual principles which opened her heart to discovery and exploration of the mystical and spiritual worlds.

She has traveled the world as a speaker and workshop facilitator on spiritual topics, and devotes her life to a path of service and love. She currently lives in Florida.

30577219R00197

Printed in Great Britain
by Amazon